Praise for *The Mindful Money Guide*

"Money may be the root of all evil, but as long as you're messing around with the stuff you might as well do it consciously and conscientiously. Marshall Glickman, simply put, will tell you how."

—Bill McKibben
Author of *The End of Nature*

"This book is a delight. 'A journey to financial health,' Glickman writes, 'starts by turning inward.' Yes, absolutely—and how wonderful to have someone say it who understands the nuts and bolts of finance as well as he. From the spiritual depths to the intricacies of selecting a socially responsible mutual fund, this book covers it all—in readable, friendly prose. A true companion for the journey to clean up one's finances—and an inspiration to do so."

—Marjorie Kelly
Publisher and Editor
Business Ethics

THE
MINDFUL
MONEY GUIDE

CREATING HARMONY BETWEEN

YOUR VALUES AND YOUR FINANCES

MARSHALL GLICKMAN

BALLANTINE WELLSPRING™
THE BALLANTINE PUBLISHING GROUP
NEW YORK

A Ballantine Wellspring™ Book
Published by The Ballantine Publishing Group

Copyright © 1999 by Marshall Glickman

www.randomhouse.com/BB/

Library of Congress Cataloging-in-Publication Data
Glickman, Marshall.
The mindful money guide : creating harmony between your values and your finances / Marshall Glickman.
p.   cm.
"Ballantine/Wellspring book."
Includes bibliographical references and index.
ISBN 0-345-43050-6 (alk. paper)
1. Finance, Personal.   I. Title.
HG179.G5517   1999
332.024—dc21   98-43543
CIP

Text design by Debbie Glasserman
Cover design by Barbara Leff
Cover illustration by Kayley LeFaiver

Manufactured in the United States of America

First Edition: May 1999

10 9 8 7 6 5 4 3 2 1

FOR MY FAMILY, MY GREATEST WEALTH

CONTENTS

PART 3: SPENDING IT

PART 4: EARNING IT

PART 5: GIVING IT AWAY

A HOLISTIC APPROACH TO MONEY

Money makes the world go 'round.

The Buddha thought it was suffering; Aristotle, happiness. Freud concluded it was sex; Woody Allen, fear of death. Four powerful drives, to be sure—all serious contenders for the title of *the* primal force, if there is such a thing. Yet while the philosophers, artists, and shrinks debate what we really want, dollars snap, crackle, and pop, dominating our thoughts and directing the traffic of the human beehive. Nothing *consciously* motivates us like money.

Money has become the focal point and organizer of our culture. It's our intimate companion, prodding us out of bed in the morning, hovering as we exchange pleasantries with our boss and negotiate outings with our kids. That we hardly notice the fiscal pull in our life only indicates its constancy. Although Marx may have failed as a prophet, he was right about economics shaping both our inner and outer landscape.

Money, after all, can literally move mountains. With a multizero bookkeeping entry, you can plug a river, turn a desert into a resort, preserve a forest, or pave it over. Outside of a bomb or a tornado, what can change the character of a neighborhood like shifting real estate values?

The flow of money affects what we read in the news, hear on the radio, and see on TV—as well as what we don't. Cash appeal speaks even louder than sex appeal. My guess is, Madonna, naked on Broadway, can't compete with a Brink's truck scattering fifties into Times Square. Pure speculation, of course, but it's backed by annual surveys indicating Americans think about money more than sex. Studies also tell us financial concerns are the leading cause of anxiety, insomnia, and divorce.

Money's shadow falls on every aspect of our lives, even the spiritual. Financial worries distract us from the vibrant present moment. Security's call stifles our creativity, keeps us plodding at tasks we'd rather forget, and cajoles us into uncomfortable compromises. If an enlightened spirit is undivided, money must be the soul's ax, cutting us off from our truest selves, turning us into hypocrites, and alienating us from friends and family. Nearly all of us have been infected with an underlying, often subtle what's-in-it-for-me? outlook to life. It's an attitude that brings bottom-line considerations to everything we do.

Money's powerful presence typically produces one of two reactions: either we become preoccupied with it, or we try to ignore it. Obviously, neither response is much of a solution. The worriers, with one eye distracted by the safe-deposit box, don't live as fully as they could. The ostriches tend to mismanage their financial affairs, enduring a subtle, nagging anxiety that can hit full force when Visa bills come due or retirement looms. Like it or not, money is something we must deal with.

The traditional prescription for personal finance has been to push for more, more, more. You can't get enough of the stuff is the underlying assumption of most money advice. One well-known money guide, for example, written by the editor of an influential financial magazine, offers the role model of a high-school dropout turned multimillionaire who got his pile by "working with a vengeance" twelve to fifteen hours a day, seven days a week, for more than thirty years. I suppose his diligence is to be admired, and few wouldn't want his bank account, but it begs the question: What kind of life did he really make for himself, his family, and the world at large?

It's a question a growing minority is asking, not as a rejection of financial freedom, but against the pressures from the Vince Lombardi school of financial planning. As former European Central Banker Bernard Lietar put it: "Money is like an iron ring we've put through our noses. We've forgotten we designed it and now it's leading us around."

In an effort to break that hold, a new breed of money books has appeared: on socially responsible investing; on the psychology and philosophy of money; on voluntary simplicity, green consuming, and right livelihood. All of these books attempt to add meaning or harmony to our financial life. Yet even the best of them address only parts of this complex issue.

Socially responsible investing (SRI) guides, for example, only cover investment-related matters, which usually lead to incomplete financial advice. SRI manuals also tend to emphasize socially responsible financial *products*, giving short shrift to other personal-finance issues, such as reducing taxes, getting a mortgage, or maximizing the effect of charitable donations. Ironically, this emphasis on SRI products even clouds the most effective ways stockholders can influence corporate policy.

The alternative money guides that address the psychological and lifestyle aspects of money tend to be long on inspiration and short on fiscal particulars.

And those titles that could loosely be classified in the penny-pinching genre are usually too restrictive for anyone but the Green Berets of cheapskates. The tightwads also overlook the subtle ways spending affects our spirit and the world. Books that claim to be planet-friendly, for example, recommend shopping at discount chains and bottom-dollar supermarkets—forgetting that these megastores rarely carry organic products and are ravaging small, independent businesses.

My point isn't to trash alternative money guides. My socially responsible investment books are dog-eared; I've read, and even reread, many of the books I'm referring to above. In some ways, *The Mindful Money Guide* is a synthesis of the best of these and other alternative works. But having surveyed and digested the whole scene, I saw the importance of a comprehensive and consistent approach that also allows plenty of choice. (Yes, sometimes the "conventional" way works best.) When it comes to a financial life, one size doesn't fit all.

So what, exactly, do I mean by a holistic approach to money? Well, several things really.

First, a holistic approach to money emphasizes quality over quantity. If used skillfully, money can enhance our life. But it easily sours if we become slaves to numbers. For example, after reading a *Worth* magazine article on retirement, you may think you need a couple mil before you can hang up your spikes. If you're disinclined to fiddle with figures yourself and are already vaguely anxious about the topic, you end up doing nothing—the goal is simply too far out of reach.

What's easy to forget is that these articles have a strong slant. Personal finance magazines earn the lion's share of their profits from advertisements for mutual funds, insurance policies, and brokerage services. While no one accuses the most respected publications of running advertorials, an ad-friendly editorial environment is a given.

Financial editors also assume their readers want to maintain their two-house, two-and-a-half cars, $90,000-plus median-income lifestyle well into their golden years. If you were never gunning for that in the first place, you need a whole other plan. You still should do some calculations—and I've included formulas that make the number crunching as easy as possible—but the figures should be based on *your* terms and assumptions. You may even find you're better off than you realized. As the Buddha would have put it if he'd been a CPA, be a financial light unto yourself.

Holistic money principle number two: Simplicity is next to godliness. Regular life is taxing enough; we don't need more stress from managing our financial affairs. Without sacrificing returns, our money life can be much simpler than what's typically advised in the business pages.

While there may be terribly clever folks who make big bucks shorting pesos and going long marks (or is it the other way around?), who wants to spend their Saturday checking on the strength of the bourse or the value of the pound or researching weather patterns in Guadalajara? Everyone wants good returns, but scouring the country to find slightly higher rates on CDs (certificates of deposit) isn't healthy—and hardly even pays. For stock investors, the extra fussing is likely to hurt returns.

Third, the Eastern mystics are right: all life is interconnected—and so are the various pieces of our financial life. Our spending patterns affect whether we can save and invest or even do work we love. Lower your tax bill and you won't have to burn the midnight monitor at the office. Put your finances in order and you can donate money and time to causes you're passionate about.

On a deeper level, this book challenges you to investigate the connections between our inherited cultural biases, your money psychology, and your money-related behaviors. If we don't recognize the money issues driving us, we'll stay in the same ruts.

Mahatma Gandhi taught that ends and means must harmonize. Work all day at a competitive, ruthless job and you won't feel abundant and peaceful when you come home, no matter how PC your investments or how big your charitable gifts. By definition, holism means that the whole is greater than the sum of its parts. To be in true financial flow, we must address all the aspects of our money life.

Fourth, the way we handle our money makes a difference. The impact of what we buy, work for, invest in, and donate to is real and creates a ripple effect. One hundred and fifty years ago, Ralph Waldo Emerson observed that the "material apparatus" a person or nation surrounds itself with reflects its state of mind and morality. "Timber, brick, lime, and stone . . . are shaped obedient to the ideas reigning in our minds." If we don't want to be buried by the shoddy, superficial, and toxic, we need to be thoughtful about our part in circulating money. Using money for positive influence isn't just the right thing to do, it's also the most rewarding. You'll feel better knowing your dollars are spent and invested truly well.

Last, but definitely not least, holistic money is about striking an appropriate balance: finding that golden mean—between a life that neither bows down to money nor neglects financial responsibilities; between getting a good return for yourself without forgetting about others; between curbing materialistic impulses without becoming austere or stingy.

An approach that seeks a proper balance, one that takes into account your life situation—thumbing its nose at "rules" sometimes and playing by them at others—doesn't make for good sound bites. It takes more skill than following a rigid program. But life itself is, if anything, complex and confusing. To carve a financial path with heart, we must negotiate seeming paradoxes with a combination of ideals, savvy with numbers, and flexibility. It's more an ongoing challenge than a solution.

Maintaining a truly healthy financial state isn't easy, but you have a much better shot at staying in that ideal zone if you develop an awareness of the forces affecting you and then make *conscious*, if difficult, choices. If nothing else, this approach has to work better than simply adopting conventional money attitudes or blindly rebelling against them.

In many ways, holistic finance is like holistic health. Both look for gentler, preventive approaches to achieve greater well-being; both recognize the damage stress inflicts; and both concede there are times standard practices still make sense.

Traditionally, doctors throw drugs at problems; financial planners, money. Like the body, money has its own laws that must be followed. You can't spend recklessly for a lifetime and expect a comfortable retirement any more than you can smoke for fifty years and expect visualizations to cure your cancer. But naturally you can't expect medical technology or a big portfolio to ensure well-being either. A fat 401(k) doesn't guarantee a fulfilling retirement any more than a good pacemaker does. Having active interests, good friends, and lifelong healthy habits are better investments. A full-spectrum approach lets you do more with what others may see as less.

This book is designed to help you imagine and achieve a financial life that more closely reflects who you really are or want to be.

There's plenty of practical advice in here—how to save for college, finance your house, invest in the stock market—things you'd expect to find in any money guide. I haven't forgotten that most of us need to stretch a dollar where possible. Yet these pragmatic concerns, filtered through a "holistic" paradigm, can offer both simpler answers, which cut through the maze of financial choices, *and* "alternative" takes on otherwise standard topics, such as "What Your Car *Really* Costs—and How Taking a Different Route Can Make You a Millionaire" or "Eleven No-Risk, High-Yielding, Tax-Free Investments That Are Good for the Planet and Would Turn Wall Street Gurus Green—with Envy."

The Mindful Money Guide is divided into five parts: "Head, Heart, and Money"; "Personal Finance"; "Spending It"; "Earning It"; and "Giving It Away." Not every part of every section may be applicable to you right now, or possibly ever. You may, for instance, really enjoy your work and not need the exercises that help you find a calling. (Although down the road, during times of self-doubt, you may want to read that material to confirm that you're on the right path.) Or perhaps now you're more concerned with getting out of debt than with giving money away. In that case, save "Setting Up a 'Poor Man's Foundation'"—a convenient, satisfying, tax-savvy way to make donations—for when your cash is more flowing.

My hope is that this book will work for your whole life, both laterally and sequentially—laterally by placing money in the context of just one part of a full life, and over time as a complete reference to financial questions as your circumstances change.

So here's to true prosperity and real wealth.

HEAD, HEART, AND MONEY

WHY LOOKING AT OUR RELATIONSHIP TO MONEY IS THE FIRST STEP ON THE ROAD TO FINANCIAL WELL-BEING

A journey to financial health doesn't begin in the accountant's office or in your den, surrounded by last year's taxes and credit card statements—unless that's where you happen to be sitting. It starts by turning inward, by looking at how you relate to money. And by seeing how money affects your relationship to nearly everything else.

Most people imagine that if they just had more, they'd stop worrying and their financial issues would disappear. So often just the opposite happens: once a person accumulates some wealth, he becomes obsessed with it—fussing with portfolios, agonizing over losses and returns, setting his sights on more expensive toys and ventures. When you have an unhealthy relationship to money, you never have enough. It's like being anorexic: the problem isn't the anorexic's body but how she feels about it. That's why losing weight doesn't improve her self-image.

True transformation comes from understanding and working on the relationship you're trying to change—whether with money, food, or a lover—rather than changing your circumstances (although that, too, may be appropriate). Once you have a healthy relationship, positive change and better results will unfold organically—even if the outcome isn't what you had originally envisioned. For example, after a chronic dieter makes peace with her body, she can concentrate on eating better and exercising. She'll become fitter and healthier without getting upset that she doesn't look anything like Twiggy—a fact that used to send her on depressive eating binges.

Achieving an ideal financial state doesn't mean earning a towering income or accumulating the "model portfolio" you read about in the business section and financial magazines. Once you've untangled your relationship to money, you'll see it's okay that you don't measure up to those standards. You'll be less likely to stretch a budget competing with showcased spenders or to abandon a modest retirement savings plan because it seems hopelessly puny. You'll feel less pressure to pursue work whose reward is mainly the salary.

Most important, whether or not a healthier relationship to money translates into a sounder fiscal condition, it should make your whole life more pleasant. Not to be bleak, but we may never get to use our retirement savings; at any time, we could get hit by that dreaded runaway truck. But feeling better about money—that, you can use immediately. Without money concerns absorbing so much thought and energy, you'll be lighter on your feet as well as your wallet.

IF EVERYONE KNOWS THAT TRUE WEALTH CAN'T BE MEASURED IN DOLLARS, WHY IS IT SO HARD TO LIVE THAT WAY?

Pity the soul who thinks the bumper sticker slogan WHO-EVER DIES WITH THE MOST TOYS WINS is a philosophy of life and not a spoof. And yet, if you're like me, walk on down the road a bit and, before you know it, you've forgotten the joke—coveting a farmhouse with pond and views, buttering up a rich uncle, or envying a friend's promotion and bonus. If we really know better, why does materialism have such a grip on us? Why is it so difficult to stop seeing the world in terms of money—who has it, who doesn't, what things cost—even when we've made a conscious decision not to do so?

Answering these questions is the first step to real change. Without understanding the forces acting on—and within—us, we're lost, unlikely ever to find our way. Looking at the place money has carved in our psyche is like looking at a map: we can see both where we are and whether alternative routes are possible—and if so, how rough those roads will be. Without this overview, we're unlikely to have the stamina and faith to stay with any path but the one we've always followed.

Social critics and alternative press columnists have traditionally blamed our rampant materialism on advertising. It does seem to be the obvious culprit: the ad industry manufactures product envy and material desires around the clock, pumping billions and billions of promotional messages into the air each year. Like acid rain, something is bound to sink in. How shocking is an epidemic of "affluenza" when the average teenager is exposed to 360,000 TV commercials before graduating from high school?

What is surprising, however, is that marketing watchdogs never truly question why advertising works. Why does seeing a sports car or deluxe Cuisinart make us want it? Pointing to quick-cut camera techniques, unshakable jingles, and fulsome models isn't enough. Consumerism spread in Eastern Europe even when commercials were illegal; nomads in the Borneo rain forest, who've never seen a television, treasure Michael Jordan T-shirts, digital wristwatches, and batteries. Even if PBS took over the world's airwaves, people would still want stuff for comfort, convenience, security, and status.

Of course, I'm not about to defend the ad industry. Advertising does turn up the materialistic heat around here and reinforces our most superficial and hedonistic qualities. I'm as happy to bash Madison Avenue as the next guy, but the politically incorrect truth is, advertising doesn't so much create desires as exploit them. We had acquisitive instincts long before Ogilvy & Mather unleashed an army of copywriters.

Spend some time with any three-year-old and we remember that no one had to teach us to be possessive and grabby. Go back even further to our first ancestors and it makes sense why that should be. By looking at our original design, it's possible to gain some insights into how money got so deeply intertwined with our psyches.

Evolutionary biologists tell us that our genetic makeup hasn't changed in forty thousand years. Our bodies and minds evolved for a life of hunting and gathering and cohabitating in small, related, nomadic groups. Our fundamental drives are the same as those that propelled our Paleolithic cousins.

In that light it's clear why three-year-olds grab stuff: it helps them make it to age four and beyond. An acquisitive instinct is a survival mechanism. Back when high tech meant flint and sharp spears, the impulse to acquire tools, weapons, and objects helped make us safer and more comfortable, with little or no downside. It's only when an overabundance of stuff is available that acquisitiveness causes problems. We're simply not designed for a world with endless consumer choice and constantly improving technology (while drawn to it at the same time).

Advanced technology and a sophisticated economy confuse many of our natural impulses. In a cash economy, money becomes the means of satisfying lots of urges: our impulse for comfort leads us to make monthly sofa payments; the desire for security is fed with IRA contributions; craving respect translates into seeking a higher-paying job. But it doesn't end there. Need to relax? That'll take a country house or a trip to the Caribbean. Got the urge to reproduce? Even that seems easier if you've got a big bankroll. So instead of paying attention to our real needs and working to fulfill them directly, we channel much of that energy into chasing money.

Not surprisingly, this doesn't work so well. Once we have the basics of food, shelter, and a modicum of possessions (which, no doubt, was all our acquisitive instinct was "meant" to accomplish), further pursuit of wealth puts us on a desire treadmill and becomes a diversion from the existential and emotional issues we face. In some ways we're more stuck in a survival mode than our earliest relatives, spending more time hunting dollars than they did chasing antelope. Anthropologists tell us that "primitive" peoples work on average two to four hours a day—leaving plenty of time for contemplation, worship, shooting the breeze with friends, and enjoying nature.

Even our built-in inclinations to share are undermined by a modern economy. For a Stone Ager, sharing was crucial for survival. Hunters needed each other—both to catch big game and for help during lean times. For Paleolithic hunters, a bad month at the office meant hunger or worse. There was no defrosting last season's mastodon to get through a dry spell. So they relied on a cousin, brother-in-law, or neighbor to pass on some of their bounty (and vice versa). Sharing was in everyone's best interest. Throughout the world, hunting and foraging peoples have strong sharing ethics and cultures.

In a developed economy, sharing is no longer obviously in your best interest. In fact, "shrewd" capitalists try to get the most they can for the least effort. The conditions that balanced sharing and selfishness in a Stone Age economy have been turned upside down, and as a result our selfish impulses are unchecked. Since we still have sharing instincts, however, it isn't surprising that we suffer guilt when we feel we aren't giving enough—and that studies show regular volunteering can improve physical health.

Trying to sort out where the influence of genetic programming ends and where the force of culture begins to shape our minds is a tricky business. What is clear is that the culture we've inherited is a strongly materialistic one. The American character was formed largely from the religious fervor of the first settlers, the Protestant work ethic, and the enterprising spirit of immigrants drawn to a land of opportunity. Meld those together and you get a culture infused with a success ethic. Benjamin Franklin articulated the country's credo in his popular *Poor Richard's Almanack* with such life-enhancing epithets as "Time is money" and "Plow deep while sluggards sleep."

In a sense, the conniving, self-promoting, and wealthy Franklin was our country's real founding father. His legacy of blending ethics, "philosophy," and wealth has been carried on by the likes of Norman Vincent Peale, Napoleon Hill, and more recently, the success motivator Tony Robbins of coal-walking fame.

The media keep the flames of the success ethic burning by doting on billionaires like Bill Gates and Warren Buffett, as if their business acumen translated into life wisdom. Money does indeed talk, and the more transient, impersonal, and homogenous our society gets, the louder it speaks. While few can compete with a Gates-sized billfold, our income, possessions, and assets take on the role of SAT scores for grownups. Net worth gets intertwined with self-worth.

To disentangle the two requires a conscious effort. Given the stacking of the genetic and cultural deck, maintaining a totally serene financial life may be impossible. But taking the edge off—making peace with money so that it loses the power to control you—is within reach.

LOOSENING
MONEY'S GRIP

Although genes and culture are powerful influences, they aren't destiny. We are still free agents, able to make choices and think for ourselves—if often in a muddled way. What we inherit are tendencies, not puppet strings. A bit of Donald Trump may live in all of us, but that doesn't suggest we build a life around materialistic urges any more than acknowledging impulses to dominate implies we should terrorize our neighborhood. Innate drives and societal expectations may be strong currents, but they can be navigated if we wish to travel in our own mindful direction.

As with most quests for health, don't look for one, permanent solution to fix your relationship with money. Instead, think ongoing challenge. And as with changing any negative ingrained habit or thought pattern, you may need to realign other parts of your life—moving the beams and walls that hold your current design in position.

This isn't the place to go into detail about well-known holistic mind/body practices, such as psychotherapy, meditation, yoga, exercise, or communing with nature, but obviously, all of these can reduce financial tension by lowering your overall stress level. Anything we do simply for the pleasure of it, anything that makes us feel more alive or causes time to drop away, undermines the power money has over us.

Unfortunately, most of us are doing the exact opposite. We let ourselves get overloaded, and workaholism creeps up on us. Our leisure time gets filled with job-related reading or financial matters that feel like work. If you spend all day manipulating numbers, then come home and study the stock market, where's your time for release—your time to engage other parts of yourself? Likewise, social workers who take on everyone's problems in the evenings and weekends are also ripe for burnout. It sounds corny, but make room for joy in your life. Plan unstructured time. It will help give perspective.

I'm certainly not recommending that you ignore financial matters. That works about as well as neglecting a leaky roof—which gives good cause to worry. Some attention to finances should be part of an overall plan to relax about money. But the idea is to create a simple, basic financial life that doesn't require much fussing with. (As already noted, much of this book is devoted to showing you how to do just that.)

BEYOND VOLUNTARY SIMPLICITY

The best-known plan for reshaping your relationship to money is voluntary simplicity—the conscious effort to limit your material life. Galvanized by Joe Dominguez and Vicki Robin's bestseller *Your Money or Your Life*, the voluntary simplicity movement has received lots of attention from hopeful environmentalists, downsized professionals, and futurists, who annually crown it as "one of the top ten trends for the upcoming decade."

What these enthusiasts never mention, however, is that voluntary simplicity is more an art than a simple decision. To really work, voluntary simplicity requires more than just tossing out TVs, rowing machines, and electric toothbrushes. Unaccompanied by a real internal shift, once the author's words of inspiration fade, all those goodies will gradually fill up the house again. Or on the opposite end, simplicity can be embraced so fervently that it turns into reverse materialism. These folks tend to watch cash outflows like a desert traveler checking his water supply and disdain anyone who consumes more than a bedouin nomad—not a good recipe for contentment.

The essence of voluntary simplicity—distinguishing between your *needs* and your *wants*—is important to developing a healthier, and ultimately more satisfying, relationship to money. But it won't work by formula. We've all met materialistic, miserly sorts with few possessions and relatively nonattached, kind ones with loads of stuff. Their shopping zeal seems to spring from a generous enthusiasm for life.

It's our underlying attitude toward money (and, of course, life itself) that matters most. Those who handle money well hold it lightly and thoughtfully. They see it not as an end in itself but for what it can do—more like embodied energy than a trophy. The meaning of any thing or object comes from what we bring to it.

The more in touch we are with our inner life (and others), the less important the outer world of things becomes. Most of us get caught up in the superficial, in the symbols of success, because we live on the surface of ourselves. We're not in touch with our deeper feelings. It's as though we were living someone else's life (or trying to, anyhow). We need to dig in deep rather than build up—or rip down, as a reverse materialist might try to do. We spend most of our time fretting about decorating when what we're really missing is a solid foundation.

The key to developing a better relationship to money is to cultivate a greater awareness of our money-related thoughts and tendencies. Then we can try to understand and work with those tendencies rather than letting them control us. The idea isn't to eliminate the desire for money and material goods but to stop confusing money with the feelings that are attached to it.

The more you know about a system—in this case yourself— the better you can operate it. Pay close attention to how you interact with money. Don't assume you know everything about yourself; observe your reactions as a scientist would.

When money-related thoughts come to mind, particularly troubling ones, write them down, noting associated thoughts and the circumstances in which they occur. Such details can clue you in to aspects of your life that require greater attention. For an obvious example, consider the likelihood that a New York investment banker will obsess about money compared to a Montana cabinetmaker. While your situation is probably somewhere in between the two, seeing a strong connection between your money worries and work can motivate change. Or perhaps you'll find that your anxieties about money are related to your parents or to certain friends. This is important information.

As Alcoholics Anonymous and other twelve-step programs have shown, the support of a like-minded community can help tremendously. You can create a healthier community for yourself by moving to a slower-paced town, switching jobs, spending less time with friends who are strongly money-oriented, and watching what you read (when I was a stockbroker, daily doses of *The Wall Street Journal* sometimes had me fantasizing about becoming a captain of industry). If none of those changes is practical, or if your money problems are beyond the everyday variety, try attending meetings sponsored by Debtors Anonymous. You don't have to be in debt to benefit from their program; Debtors Anonymous meetings provide a forum to discuss any money problem.

THE FOUR MONEY TYPES

Being hip to your usual response to money can help you rescript and rehearse healthier behavior. Psychologists who specialize in resolving money issues speak of four fundamental money personalities: spenders, haters, hoarders, and chasers. Naturally, these simple characterizations don't recognize the complexity in every personality. Still, most of us veer toward one or the other type—even while recognizing parts of ourself in the other categories.

Spenders are those who buy beyond their means—in extreme cases accumulating huge credit card debt. They need to look closely at the connection between shopping and mood so they don't abuse shopping as others might alcohol or drugs.

Hoarders need to recognize that clinging to money because they fear poverty actually creates the daily *experience* of poverty. Often what underlies these worries is a general need for control and an inability to be comfortable with uncertainty.

Money haters, who believe that money is the root of all evil, tend to create deprived conditions. They need to see that undergoing a monthly struggle to pay the rent doesn't help anybody or make the world a better place. In a subliminal way, money haters may be trying to harm themselves, re-creating unpleasant experiences they had in childhood.

Money chasers are those who put a big premium on ac-quiring a fortune. They are often hiding insecurity—using money to compensate for inadequacies in other parts of life that can't be measured so easily.

All money types should try to explore the feelings *behind* their money-centered thoughts. Anxiety and depression are common reactions to financial matters, but anxiety and de-pression are often masking scarier emotions. The real ques-tion is, what's causing the anxiety and depression? Is it the specter of an uncomfortable old age, burdensome expecta-tions of parents, "losing" an unconscious competition with a sibling, or the loss of independence?

Pay close attention when anxious and uncomfortable feel-ings arise and see what's happening in your body. Try to experience your emotions nonverbally, not attempting to change them or wish you were feeling something else. This may be difficult when you're in the grip of anxiety since the worried thoughts can keep you preoccupied. If you're having a hard time moving past the anxious thoughts, ask yourself, "If I weren't feeling anxiety right now, what would I be feel-ing?" Don't try to repress or deny anxious feelings, but asking that question can sometimes give a peek at your underlying emotions.

If your money thoughts tend to center around wanting more, ask yourself if there is anything else that could help alleviate the lack you're feeling. It's not uncommon to confuse the need for respect, love, or fulfilling work with the need for more money. As novelist James Buchan phrased it, "money is frozen desire." Thawing out those desires and exploring them can give insight into why money really motivates us. It can also take away some of its power. It's often helpful to look at how your parents handled money and how that made you feel.

Don't expect a crashing breakthrough to defuse all your money issues—dramatic psychological insights are far more common in Hitchcock movies and TV psychodramas than in real life. Usually, when we're "stuck" or troubled by something, there are multiple causes to sort through. Developing healthier responses to money is likely to happen gradually, in fits and starts—partly from self-knowledge and partly from a willingness to just be comfortable with our discomfort. Of course even after gaining some insight into your reactions to money, you still have the difficult task of remaining untangled while in the midst of the stresses and distractions of everyday life.

The Buddhist practice of *tonglen* meditation—which means "taking in and sending out"—can be helpful to work with painful or disorienting feelings. When unwanted emotions come up—say, the fear of being destitute when you're old—rather than trying to push that pain away or quickly distracting yourself with another thought (or by going shopping), turn it into a meditation. "Breathe in" the scary feelings. In other words, stay with uncomfortable emotions without resisting them. This may seem odd at first as it's the opposite of our usual reaction, but by accepting unpleasant feelings, we take away some of their power, soften our defenses (which typically cause more trouble than the actual pain we're resisting), and develop compassion for ourselves (and thus, ultimately, for others). Eventually you'll find it's possible to be aware of your fears without being dominated by them or closing down.

When breathing out, visualize and try to sense a white, cool light. See if you can radiate this healing light from every pore as you send it out. This "light" gives one a sense of spaciousness and openness which is normally missing when we just stew or boil—which tends to solidify and strengthen our negative feelings. Working with your in and out breaths in this fashion gives you something "concrete" to do when struggling, without denying or repressing your difficult emotions.

USING VISUALIZATIONS: PROSPERITY CONSCIOUSNESS, *UNTWISTED*

Most books, and now Web sites, that mix money, mood, and metaphysics ask us to cultivate what's known as "prosperity consciousness." What exactly is meant by the term can vary somewhat from author to author (or Web master to Web master), but it usually involves a few elements: First, developing a state of mind that sees life as abundant and generous. Second, by doing that, wealth will naturally flow to you. Third, the tools for creating such a mind-set are affirmations and visualizations.

If you're curmudgeonly, as I am, your first instinct will be to dismiss prosperity consciousness as a New Age gimmick. I kept picturing Marin County stockbrokers rubbing hundred-dollar bills against crystals for clairvoyant market picks. To me, it sounded like an exotic name for wishful thinking.

While I may be a stick-in-the-mud, there actually is good reason for skepticism. A number of self-proclaimed spiritual gurus (and a few outright hucksters) have packaged "prosperity consciousness" with New Age accoutrements essentially to sell books, tapes, and seminars. Their message boils down to "Create the right vibe, and Texas-sized cash flow will head your way." If that sounds too good to be true, it's because it is. No one gets rich from this approach, except maybe the prosperity coach. Follow their program—shelling out for retreats, subliminal tapes, and tithing to your "counselor"—and even if you didn't need good fortune before starting their courses, you will when you're done.

But cut out the profit motives, ego trips, and naïve thinking and you'll find that a couple of tools associated with prosperity consciousness (namely, visualizations and creating a sense of financial well-being) can work. It is possible to re-program unhealthy beliefs so you *feel* richer.

When you think about it, this shouldn't be that hard. We are, after all, basically quite affluent. Take a quick scan of how most of the world lives or how most humans have lived throughout history and you get some perspective. Pretty soon you'll be wondering why you ever felt deprived or anxious about money. What's standing between us and a feeling of prosperity is misperception. Clear those thoughts away and you'll immediately feel better.

Before words existed, people thought in images. And it's likely that after language emerged, our earliest ancestors didn't separate dreams, spirits, and visions from "rational" thought the way we do. Even now, our dreams and memories are conveyed mostly in pictures. Imagery is the language of the unconscious.

Conscious visualizations work to reprogram our unhealthy, unconscious impressions *before* they become thoughts. Experiments show that imagining something can have an effect similar to actually viewing it (the obvious example of this is a sexual fantasy). This at least partially explains why active imaging works: when you imagine something to be true, associated chemical reactions occur, priming your mind/body for that reality. It's been clinically proved that visualizations can affect "involuntary" bodily functions such as white blood cell counts.

Visualization exercises, used in combination with biofeedback techniques (which help access the nonverbal parts of the brain), have produced some dazzling results—including curing chronic alcoholism, depression, anorexia, and multiple-personality disorders. Similar methods could be used to create a healthy relationship to money.

This is how you do it: Imagine yourself responding to money as you ideally would like to. If you're a hoarder who's pained by parting with a buck, visualize yourself as generous. Picture your generosity as vividly as possible in a situation that would normally make you feel tight; see it happening in the present moment. If you're a spender who has trouble holding on to money, you could picture yourself walking past your favorite store, unperturbed—or even pleased to be empty-handed. These particular images might not work for you, so create your own. The idea is to envision yourself feeling prosperous and at peace with money, however you see it.

It may take some practice at first. Try to temporarily suspend any doubts or disbelief.

The clinical success of combining visualizations with biofeedback indicates the importance of repetition and creating images in a deeply relaxed, dreamlike state. Try doing the exercises just before falling asleep at night and while waking up and still groggy in the morning. The more vivid the images, the better—and repeat them daily for at least a month. Of course, it can't hurt to think of them during the day, particularly if you're feeling anxious about your finances.

If nothing else, visualizations work as vivid personal mission statements, reaffirmed every day. They can help keep us focused on bringing about the change we imagine is possible. The first—and hardest—part of a financial makeover is changing our reaction to money. By contrast, the mechanics of personal finance, the actual handling of greenbacks, is fairly easy.

PART 2

PERSONAL FINANCE

IN THE GARDEN OF
PERSONAL FINANCE

In many ways, learning to manage your money is like learning to garden. Before grabbing a hoe—or a hot issue—you should get some seasoned advice. That's why the first chapter in this part, "The Cosmic Laws of Money," offers what I see as the seven commandments of personal finance. These guidelines are, in essence, all the money advice you ever really need. Heeding them will create a sound financial life—and is likely to do you more good than reading a wheelbarrowful of technical manuals.

Once you know these basics, then comes the unglamorous groundwork: in the case of finances, that's storing some cash in the bank, picking insurance, and tending to things like your taxes and your home's energy efficiency. When those are taken care of, you can plant stocks and/or bonds for future gains and then—hardest of all—wait for them to bear fruit. Of course, if you want to be an organic gardener or investor, yields aren't your only consideration.

Like organic gardening, mindful investing feels more rewarding than the conventional way; it also takes more sensitivity and sometimes more effort. Usually, however, it actually makes things easier by eliminating gadgets and options that ultimately aren't productive anyway. For that reason, you won't see every financial tool covered—or even mentioned—in the pages that follow. Many financial instruments—such as commodities, equity options, or even annuities—are either losing propositions or only worthwhile for professionals. So why learn about them? At a time when bank certificates of deposit (CDs) come in more flavors than Baskin Robbins ice cream, a pared-down investing menu blissfully simplifies the tending of your financial garden.

Despite all the hullabaloo, the fundamentals of managing money haven't changed. The laws of risk and return remain the same as when the first brokers set up under the old buttonwood tree near Wall Street. Sticking to the basics and tempering them with holistic considerations can create a financial life with minimal stress, one that produces good returns and makes the world a better place—without requiring capital letters after your name.

THE COSMIC LAWS OF MONEY

Every game has its own rules. And so it goes with money. Even if there isn't an official handbook, financial "laws" exist, governing money's ebb and flow and creating outcomes we must deal with—regardless of their inconvenience or unfairness.

Understanding the fundamental principles of personal finance is the first step to surviving, even enjoying, the game of money. It's amazing that most people wouldn't play a game of Ping-Pong without knowing the house rules but never bother finding out how money works and affects them.

Throughout your adult life, you've probably bumped into bits and snatches of helpful money advice and hardly noticed. We're so inundated with tips, it's hard to know which to pay attention to and which to ignore. And since most financial advice comes packaged with ear-numbing jargon or saccharine prose, you probably just tuned it out.

The good news is, to handle money well, you need only master a few basic, relatively simple principles. Of course, as with most games, you could spend a lifetime honing your skills and learning the nuances of the sport, but that's completely optional. Focusing on a handful of essentials can keep your finances in fine shape with a minimum of effort—

allowing the latest financial products and news to happily pass you by.

No matter how spiritually advanced or ethical you are, ignoring these money laws means fighting financial gravity. Heed them and you can go with the flow.

The Relativity of Numbers. "Financial independence," wrote former *Fortune* magazine editor Marshall Loeb in one of his popular money guides, "means having the wherewithal to say to yourself: 'If I wanted to, I could quit what I'm doing today and live comfortably for the rest of my life.'" When Mr. Loeb wrote those words, you can be sure he imagined a net worth with many zeros to the right of it.

Almost 150 years before Loeb's book existed, Henry David Thoreau arrived at the same conclusion, except Thoreau determined that financial independence could be achieved with a few months' wages and a willingness to forgo conveniences. "A man is rich in proportion to the things he can afford to let alone," observed Thoreau.

And there you have the two main roads—heading in opposite directions—to financial security: build a large pile to indulge your desires or manage your urges so you don't need much. Naturally, in between those two extremes one can cut an infinite number of paths mixing restraint and indulgence. The combination you choose should be a result of your circumstances, who you are, what you value, and how you feel about your work. (If, for example, you don't want to quit working in the first place, you don't need a large portfolio to replace your income.) The point is to think about what *you* require and then act accordingly—and not just be whipped around by others' expectations or cultural messages at large.

A financial plan, even a vague one, should begin with a realistic assessment of how you want to live. Thoreau's simplicity may be too spartan for you. After all, some of life's pleasures—front-row ballet seats, gourmet Italian restaurants, and a back porch overlooking the California coast—happen to be expensive. Even those with more modest tastes may want therapy, a far-flung trip, or music lessons—each of which can require some dough. Are these worth sacrificing for financially? And if so, how much sacrifice? Only you can make those decisions, and the clearer you are about them, the clearer it will be how you need to organize your finances.

The Art of Budgeting. The hardest part of personal finance isn't understanding the intricacies of stocks and bonds, learning the ins and outs of estate planning, or outwitting the IRS (although all these can come in handy); it's developing good habits, having patience, and exercising spending discipline.

The art of budgeting is learning how to make due with less than you take in. It's about accepting limits. If your "in"-box isn't consistently bigger than your "out"-box, your financial life will become messy—and you'll never be putting anything aside for the proverbial rainy day.

Roughly one out of ten people doesn't need a budget. They're naturally frugal. Money clings to them like a wet T-shirt, and they can't understand the fuss. The only reason they may need a budget is if they are excessively tight and want to bring a healthier balance of spending into their life (see the chapter entitled "The Yin/Yang Spending Solution").

The rest of the population needs a budget—some more desperately than others. In fact, those who bristle or wilt at the idea probably need it most. The best strategy for these folks is to use automatic deductions: either have your employer put part of your paycheck (10 percent is ideal) toward a retirement plan or have a mutual fund make monthly withdrawals from your bank account (many funds do this for no extra cost). Managing with what's left after the deductions in effect becomes your budget.

If you'd like to be more scientific about the process than that, figuring a budget is a good discipline. It requires you to think about your priorities.

Start by recording your total after-tax income. Then note all your normal expenses. As personal finance writer Andrew Tobias says, this is like naming all the states. At the first pass, you'll remember about forty-three; with some real effort, you'll get up to forty-eight; but to find those missing two, you'll need to sneak a look at the map.

In this case, the map is your checkbook, bank statement, and credit card account(s). Go through them and divvy expenses up according to category. This may seem too prosaic for an advanced soul like yourself, but remember, small leaks sink big ships. "Little" expenses add up. A night out—dinner and movie, followed by drink or dessert, and baby-sitter—easily costs $90 to $100. Nothing wrong with that, but if you do it every week, it's a $5,000-a-year after-tax expense. Done twice a week and ten Gs have walked out the door—before you've paid rent or bought the kids a glass of milk.

Some pleasures, of course, should be built into your budget or you'll feel as if you were wearing a corset. Still, seeing a full accounting of all your entertainment costs can be a great motivator to trim back.

Part of what makes living within our means so hard is the difficulty of adjusting to inflation. If you grew up thinking $50,000 a year meant you had "made it" and $100 bought a station wagon full of groceries, you'll instinctively assume that certain "basics" *should* go with those income numbers—

forgetting that price tags have grown with you. A $30,000 salary just doesn't buy what we feel it should. So to get a realistic grip on the numbers, we need to see them plainly laid out before us.

Goals are the key to sticking with a budget. Otherwise, you simply feel as if you're punishing yourself. On any given night, there's little reason to say no to an evening out. After all, what's another ninety bucks? But when you make a plan, when you see not only why you need to say no sometimes but how you can build toward something else if you do, saying no makes sense. Play Pictionary once a month with friends instead, and you'll be on the road to savings.

As with dieting, be realistic or you'll give up before you reap the benefits. If you have small children and want to cut back on your work hours, don't figure on saving anything right now. If you're in debt, make erasing the negative numbers your first priority—and forget about the burgeoning portfolio until next year.

It's easier to cut back on your spending if you keep a few things in mind:

First, remember all the good stuff you already have, and haven't been appreciating. Cutting back on new purchases gives you a chance to get reacquainted with your old pals (Van Morrison still sounds good twenty years later).

Second, no matter how much you make, you'll want more. Some people get by on less than you do, and others go bankrupt with much more.

Last, don't forget that the restraint is for your own benefit. Saying no because you can't afford something is one thing, but saying "pass" because you *want* to—because you've got a goal—that's a whole nother story. Most people make the mistake of buying things low on their priority list and end up unable to afford what they really want most. That's real deprivation.

Once you set a budget, the truly tedious part is finding out if you're sticking to it. To track your expenses, you can use a computer program, budget book, or some lined scrap paper stapled together. It doesn't really matter as long as you record all your expenditures and compare them to your plan. (Actually, since you're turning over a new leaf, you may want to bypass the expensive software.)

Many personal finance advisers recommend keeping detailed spending records for your whole life. Unless you've got serious spending issues (or are a frustrated accountant), that sounds excessive to me. But do record expenses for at least one week for every year you've been alive. (It took a lifetime to develop your current habits, so it will take some time to change them.) After serving your record-keeping sentence, you will have developed an intuitive sense of appropriate spending. If your financial circumstances change, do another budget to readjust to your new situation.

Debt. Debt is a double-edged sword. To avoid getting cut, remember a simple, two-part rule: It's fine to borrow for investments that are likely to appreciate (such as a house, an education, or a business), but avoid borrowing for things that depreciate (cars, clothing, furniture, vacations, etc.).

While stocks, over time, may fall into the appreciating assets column, borrowing heavily against your portfolio is flirting with disaster. Sharp downturns can wipe you out, even if the market bounces back later. For your average dabbler, it's a mistake—and likely to cost you not only in savings but in worry.

Taking on debt creates a long-term obligation not to be

taken lightly. In case your mom hasn't warned you, be suspicious of the easy credit that's thrown at you by credit card companies. One in every hundred households files for bankruptcy each year, many from towering credit card bills. The real price of excessive debt is anxiety, pressure to work at the highest-paying job you can get (regardless of whether you like it), and buying into a cycle of financial stress that keeps you on a treadmill, hustling just to pay for your things.

Know Thy Hidden Enemies. The penalties in the money game are hidden, making them easy to overlook. Ask someone how much he makes and he'll rarely answer with an after-tax number. Rarer still is someone who would or could tell you her wage after deducting her costs and time for commuting, day care, clothing, midtown lunches, and so forth. After subtracting all job-related costs and factoring in the extra hours of commuting and preparing for work, a $10-an-hour gig may net less than $7 per. Too often, we protect our egos at the expense of our financial health by imagining we make our gross pay.

Financial planner Ginger Applegarth says a good rule of thumb is to multiply the price of any potential purchase by 1.63 to get your before-*tax* cost (that calculation would look even worse if you included not just taxes but the whole shebang of associated work costs). In that light, frivolous spending looks really expensive, and things like mowing your own lawn look good (and if you do it briskly with a human-powered engine, it can even count as exercise—one less reason to buy a health club membership).

For investments, the unseen costs to be aware of are taxes and inflation. Assume, for example, that someone in the 28 percent tax bracket earns 5 percent in a money market account while inflation is 3 percent. After taxes and inflation take their cut, the investment nets just .6 percent (a numbers example: the $1,000 pays $50 in interest minus the $30 loss of buying power and $14 in taxes—netting $6). Using tax-deferred retirement accounts and holding stock in good companies (over the long run) helps you stay ahead of inflation and taxes.

Risk. Investing and risk go together like tamales and spice. It can't be avoided. While most people know this, when I was a broker, I was regularly surprised by new investors who expected *guaranteed* high returns.

Even so-called safe investments such as bank CDs, while protecting your principal, carry the risk of losing value from the effects of inflation. Stocks, which offer excellent returns over time, can be hazardous to your wealth in the short term.

The best you can do is manage risk, which entails finding the right balance between your circumstances, emotional temperament, and diversified investments. (See the section "Where to Put Your Investment Dollars" for details.)

The Value of Time. Even if the wealthy didn't bend the ears and hearts of politicians, the rich would still get richer. Money makes money, and over time compounding returns can turn small investments into really big ones. To take a famous example, remember that $24 in wampum for which Manhattan was "sold" in 1626? If those 24 bucks had been invested and reinvested for 8 percent returns (roughly the average performance of the stock market since records have been kept), it would have been worth $64.8 trillion in 1998.

You probably aren't planning to hold your investments for 372 years, but compounding can still work its wizardry for you. Hold off buying a car, invest those funds in an average-performing stock mutual fund, and seven years later you can buy a cottage outright or have a big down payment for a house.

Understand What You Invest In. No one can foresee the future or accurately predict fluctuations in the stock market, but you should always understand the risks, goals, and costs of any investment you make. Most investments are sold by salespeople whose interests aren't fully aligned with yours. Know how—and how much—a salesperson is getting paid for his or her "advice." Commissions come out of your pocket.

Managing money comes with responsibility; trust no one blindly. A sound bite overheard from a financial guru won't give you enough conviction to hang in through an economic downturn. Neither will a tip from your neighbor—or even a bunch of neighbors. If anything, if everyone is talking up an investment, it may be a good reason to sell or stay away since all the buyers are probably already in.

BEFORE OPENING THE BUSINESS PAGES

CASH CUSHIONS AND WHERE TO KEEP THEM

Before investing a farthing in that ecofriendly car wash your cousin promises can't miss or even putting a penny into the stock market, you should put aside enough cash—liquid, safe, readily spendable money—to cover roughly six months of living expenses. There is an amazing array of options for parking your cash. Nearly everyone is familiar with the most common: checking, passbook savings, money market funds, and certificates of deposit (CDs). There are also T-bills, short-term municipal and corporate bonds, bond funds, and cash management accounts, which combine a brokerage account with checking, credit card, and money market. Despite the large menu, deciding what to do with your short-term money is quite simple.

You probably have a fairly good grasp on your regular expenses and know how much to keep in checking to meet your monthly nut. Beyond that, try to keep at least a few thousand dollars in a money market, which is totally liquid, in case your furnace or car collapses. If you see no big expenses on the near-term horizon, buy a CD, as it usually gives a better return. CDs, which are federally insured up to

$100,000 per account, per bank, are available in a variety of maturity expirations—from three months to five years. Withdrawing the money early usually requires that you forfeit some interest.

Interest rates on short-term investments tend to be highly competitive. For most of us, good ol' banks offer all we need for our short-term money. Someone in a high tax bracket can perhaps squeeze a slightly better after-tax yield from a *tax-free* money market account or short-term municipal bond, but usually it's hardly worth the hassle (unless we're talking real big numbers). Ditto for short-term U.S. government debt instruments such as T-bills. Besides, many socially conscious investors aren't pleased with how the U.S. government spends its/our money.

To make the biggest social impact with your short-term savings, keep it at a socially conscious bank or a credit union, which tends to lend its money to small businesses and homeowners in the community.

CHOOSING YOUR BANK

Most people don't think of their bank as a catalyst for social change. Yet if you accept the money-makes-the-world-go-round premise, to whom a bank lends will influence which way we spin. So while your neighbor's bank may finance a new strip mall or oil well, yours could be helping an organic farm get on its feet.

Socially responsible banking first received national attention in the mid-seventies when Chicago's South Shore Bank turned a poor, decaying section of Chicago into a respectable area with pleasant housing and thriving shops. South Shore performed its "miracle" simply by investing in the very neighborhoods it took deposits from—and from socially concerned savers throughout the country who got wind of its intentions. It was a reversal of the illegal but still routine practice called "redlining"—taking depositors' money from poor areas but not lending it back to those same people.

In 1977, partly to address the redlining problem, Congress passed the Community Reinvestment Act (CRA), which was created to encourage banks to meet the credit needs of their local communities, including those in low- and moderate-income areas. Every bank has a CRA rating, which is made public. You can get a copy of your own bank's rating by contacting its main office.

However, there are two problems with CRA ratings. First, as John Lind, executive director of the banking watchdog group CANICCOR, points out, "CRA reports tend to give almost everyone a 'satisfactory' rating, overemphasizing banks' efforts to establish monitoring systems and 'community relations,' which includes their advertising. The actual distribution of loans is underanalyzed." Groups such as CANICCOR have developed their own methods of analyzing lending patterns and can provide independent appraisals of your bank's lending fairness (see listing in the appendix).

Second, simply filing CRA reports doesn't mean a bank is sensitive to local concerns. Large commercial banks think and invest on a large scale. They tend to be removed from the real needs of smaller communities and are environmentally insensitive.

When there's a choice between a small, local bank and a large commercial one, stick with the regional bank. As a rule, money held by your regional bank is more likely to be reinvested back into your area. As those familiar with the basics of bioregionalism know, the more economically self-sufficient a region is, the healthier it is fiscally and environmentally and the more responsive it will be to local social justice issues.

Long before South Shore Bank inspired feature articles across the country, credit unions had been practicing a brand of community banking. Credit unions are federally insured, nonprofit, tax-exempt financial cooperatives that essentially act like banks. They exist solely to serve their members—which can be organized by a variety of criteria, from union members or location to sexual orientation. The bulk of a credit union's deposits are invested in loans to its members, strengthening the community the credit union serves. While even some regional banks resell mortgage loans (although not necessarily deposits) to larger institutions (meaning your funds enter the great global financial community in the sky), credit unions typically do not.

Community-development credit unions are a socially proactive form of credit union, designed to help disadvantaged communities. Sometimes socially motivated depositors are willing to accept a lower-than-market interest rate so more of their funds can be channeled into socially productive developments. With more than 15,000 credit unions in the United States (300-plus of those are the community-development variety), even country folk usually have a local socially appealing banking option.

If you want your banking dollars to benefit the environment, you need a traditional but progressive bank such as Vermont National (its socially responsible division), Wainwright Bank & Trust Company, or ShoreBank Pacific, the nation's first fully dedicated ecobank. Located in an area of

Washington State's temperate rain forest that has been suffering from high unemployment, ShoreBank Pacific uses its deposits to assist environmentally sustainable businesses such as oyster growers, cranberry farmers, and environmentally conscientious lumber companies.

For those who want to address specific social issues, there are plenty of choices—such as women-, minority-, or Native American–owned banks. Each is sensitive to its constituency. The National Bankers Association provides a list of specialty banks (see appendix).

If you don't live near a socially or environmentally sensitive bank, you can keep your checking account at a credit union or small regional bank and send your longer-term savings to an institution whose lending practices more closely match your goals.

PC CHECKS

The last—and yes, least—socially conscious banking detail to consider is your checks. Checks ordered through your bank tend to be more expensive and printed on *non*recycled paper. Using an unaffiliated printer saves both a little tree and cash (see appendix).

INSURANCE: A LITTLE KNOW-HOW WILL PROTECT YOUR ASS(ETS) AND SAVE MONEY

Caveat number one: Don't discuss insurance with your friends or neighbors—unless you wish to free up your social calendar. This prohibition, however, doesn't mean you should neglect the topic. Unfortunately, this is exactly what most people do. Research by the nonprofit National Insurance Consumer Organization reveals that more than 90 percent of Americans have both the wrong types and amounts of insurance.

Accidents and horror stories do indeed happen—which is why you need insurance. But in the wrong mouth, these tales of woe generate sales commissions instead of appropriate coverage. Since most people don't know what they really need to protect themselves, they are vulnerable to a salesperson's scare tactics, emotional manipulation, and biased, company-produced charts that stack the deck in favor of the policy being sold. So while you may not be excited about insurance per se, you should familiarize yourself with some basics. The right insurance is not only likely to provide better protection than you have now, it may very well cost less.

A PRIMER

The first consideration is, do you really need insurance? Contrary to insurance company pep rallies and industry PR, not everyone does. Life insurance, for example, is for those who have dependents. If no one else relies on your income, you don't need it. Likewise, sometimes it's unnecessary to buy your own health and disability insurance—say, after you retire and are sufficiently covered by Medicare, Medicaid, and Social Security or you have an independent income.

Guideline number two is to purchase only broad coverage. Avoid those single-issue policy offers—like flight, appliance, cancer, hospital stay, and even dental insurance (unless a good group plan is available at work). As a general rule, if a policy comes to your attention via junk mail or a restaurant foyer brochure, ignore it.

Stick to the biggies that cover most catastrophes: life, disability, and health. Homeowner's insurance makes that short list if you own a home. And many financial planners consider liability coverage essential, particularly if have a lot of assets or own a business that increases your vulnerability to lawsuits. Shunning "inexpensive," single-issue policies as well as riders on traditional ones will help you afford the essentials.

There are a few things you can do to reduce insurance costs and paperwork. One is to take a high deductible; that is, rather than have your insurance kick in after the first $100 or $250 of losses, have your coverage begin at $500, $1,000, or even a few thousand dollars. Raising your deductible even several hundred dollars can often save 15 to 20 percent per year on premiums; go even higher and the savings really kick in. Obviously, you're betting you'll be healthy and accident-free for at least a few years, but the odds are with you (instead of the insurance company)—and you'll save the time and aggravation of filing for small claims. Assuming you've got some savings, why pay someone to take on a risk you can afford yourself?

The second way to save on insurance is to shop around. Since insurance has little sex appeal, you might expect premiums to be consistent and competitive, like money market rates. 'Tain't so. Rates vary widely.

If you have a good relationship with a knowledgeable insurance agent and feel she serves your best interests, by all means stick with her. But that's not usually the case. It's hard for insurance salespeople to stay objective since they're compensated purely by commissions.

After getting a grasp on your insurance needs (see the following subsections), consider calling discount or low-load insurers, which offer significantly reduced rates. At this writing, there are no socially responsible insurance companies, so you needn't worry about possible moral versus price dilemmas and can shop for the best price guilt free. Most insurance companies tend to invest mostly in U.S. government bonds; so except for the portion that is funding B-52 retrofits and mining subsidies, the money is generally used for benign purposes.

As a general rule, getting insurance through your employer (especially if it's a large one) reduces your cost. The only exception to this is life insurance. Since group plans are insured under average health and mortality rates, if you're healthier than average, you can usually find a better rate on your own.

DISABILITY INSURANCE

You've probably heard the statistics: more than a third of us between the ages of thirty and sixty-five will be disabled for at least three months. Or put another way, you're seven times more likely to become disabled before you retire than to die.[1] We usually react to that information by filing it in the "it-won't-happen-to-me" part of the brain: protection against disability is the most common gap in people's insurance coverage.

Ask yourself how long you could pay your bills and maintain some approximation of your lifestyle if you couldn't work. If the answer is "not very long," you need disability insurance. For most of us, our most valuable financial asset is

1. Both those figures are considerably smaller for the white-collared.

our future earnings. Take those away, and we're financial toast. Bills don't stop coming just because we can't go to work. In fact, they usually increase.

You should have enough disability insurance to cover 60 to 70 percent of your income. Be prepared to pay up, as disability protection is expensive. Group plans usually cost less, so investigate acquiring it through an organization or a professional association you're a member of. You can also mitigate the cost somewhat by tailoring it to your needs. If you have a spouse who works, for example, you need less coverage. Ditto if you plan to retire soon or have a well-off mother-in-law willing and waiting in the wings. Remember, the acid-test question is: How will you manage without your current income?

LIFE INSURANCE

Life insurance is the bread and butter for insurance salesmen. Trained like Navy Seals, their mission is to sell you large, whole-life policies. This is fine if you need such a policy, but odds are, you don't.

As already noted, if you don't have any financial dependents—which usually means pre–college-age children—skip to another section, as you don't need life insurance, period.

To figure your insurance needs, you must calculate how much of your income you would have to replace and for how long (should you perish). Keep in mind that after you're gone—with fewer concert tickets and containers of Ben & Jerry's to buy—family expenses will go down somewhat. Usually, replacing 75 percent of your annual income will be sufficient (make that 80 percent if you don't make much now and 60 percent if you pull in a big salary).[2]

Use the following chart to figure the gross amount of insurance you need.

YEARS OF INCOME TO REPLACE	MULTIPLY AFTER-TAX INCOME BY[3]
5	4.7
10	9.0
15	12.0
20	15.0
25	18.0
30	20.0

From that total, consider the following adjustments:

1. Take into account the money-handling personalities of your survivors. If your spouse is hopelessly incompetent with the green stuff, throw in extra insurance for good measure.

2. Round up roughly six months' worth of income to pay for the illness and funeral expenses that accompany most deaths.

3. If you want to guarantee that your child's college education is paid for and you don't have other provisions, add

2. If your surviving spouse earns less than $20,000 a year, he or she will get monthly income from Social Security. (For more details about exact benefits, contact the Social Security Administration at [800] 772-1213.) Subtract the amount your spouse will receive from Social Security from the projected annual total you'll need.

3. This assumes that your heirs invest your insurance proceeds for an annual return of 3 percent over and above inflation and taxes.

an appropriate amount to your total (for details, see "The College-Funding Challenge," on page 129).

4. Subtract savings and benefits that will come from retirement accounts, work pension plans, or other investments you have. This means rich folks rarely need life insurance, unless they have a liquidity problem with their estate.

THE TERM VERSUS CASH VALUE DEBATE

The squabble in question is whether to get term insurance or a policy that accumulates cash value. The latter type takes a variety of forms—with names such as whole life, ordinary life, universal, or variable. These combine life insurance coverage with a savings and investment plan. Part of your premiums go to insurance and part to building reserves. Cash-value policies are very popular with insurance salespeople as they pay juicy commissions.

Actually, there shouldn't be much debate about which type of policy to buy. Nearly every financial expert—who doesn't sell insurance—maintains that term is the way to go (unless you have a large estate and will need protection against hefty estate taxes; see Part 5, "Giving It Away," for details).

Term insurance is quite simple: it pays your beneficiaries if you die. It is pure insurance, working much like homeowner's or auto insurance, which only kicks in when a disaster does. When the term you've paid for expires (policies are typically sold in one-, five-, ten-, fifteen-, etc., year increments), so does your insurance. For that reason, buy only a *guaranteed renewable* policy—just in case your health deteriorates.

Term insurance typically costs one-fifth to one-eighth as much as cash-value policies. By taking the difference between the two plans and investing it yourself, you'll end up with more savings—the benefit of avoiding the administrative costs, commissions, and investment manager fees that would otherwise reduce your returns.

Point this out to an agent and he or she will say, "Sounds great, but will you really do it?" Cash-value insurance can indeed work as a forced savings plan. And you should consider it for that reason if you know you won't end up investing the difference. Do make sure, however, that you can keep up with the payments: the extra cost of cash-value policies means that many can't afford them over time. Roughly 25 percent of these policies lapse after only a few years—preventing any reserves from building up, leaving you with nothing (which costs much more). A better way to discipline yourself with enforced savings is to set up automatic deductions at work or have a mutual fund take monthly contributions from your bank account.

HEALTH INSURANCE

While controversy and frustration over national health insurance—or the lack thereof—is likely to continue long after this book is otherwise out of date, one thing remains certain: hospital stays are hazardous to your financial health. Even minor injuries can rack up nosebleeding bills. This makes health insurance an expensive must-have.

There are, as already noted, a few ways to reduce the cost. For starters, try to get covered through your job or your spouse's. If that's not an option, investigate group plans through any organizations and associations you're affiliated with. Do a thorough job shopping around—and don't overlook health maintenance organizations (HMOs).

If you're basically healthy, maintain a high deductible.

While you'll curse my name if you hit a patch of bad health, a high deductible usually offers considerable savings in the long run. High deductibles dramatically reduce premiums and still protect you against catastrophe. Obviously, if you expect some kind of major medical care—say, if you're pregnant or about to have a knee operation—now isn't the time for a high deductible.

When paying your own medical costs, be especially vigilant about double-checking your bills. Most hospitals and doctors assume you are covered by insurance and blithely charge you as much as possible. When I broke my collarbone, for example, one doctor charged me $760 (above and beyond other hospital bills) for about 7½ minutes of his time. If you factored in his drive to the hospital, the whole excursion probably took him about half an hour. When I asked his office manager how the doctor justified his hourly rate and pointed out that I was paying for this myself (my family health insurance has a $2,200 deductible), she immediately cut the bill in half. Of course, everyone should object to overcharging, as it ultimately adds to all our costs, but this isn't just theory when it comes out of your own pocket.

One study found that 96 percent of hospital bills had errors—74 percent of which were in the hospital's favor. Monitor your tab. Record everything that's done in a notebook. When you're staying overnight, ask for a copy of the previous day's bill in the morning. It should include details of charges for medication and services. Reviewing it when events are fresh in your mind will help you catch mistakes before they show up on the bill.

ELEVEN NO-RISK, HIGH-YIELDING, TAX-FREE INVESTMENTS THAT ARE GOOD FOR THE PLANET AND WOULD TURN WALL STREET GURUS GREEN—WITH ENVY

Throughout the 1980s and into the 1990s, the stock market had its best fifteen-year performance ever—returning roughly 16 percent annually. During that time (and at any other time, for that matter), most money managers didn't match that record. Consequently, any man, woman, or child who has consistently bested 16 percent annual returns is pedestaled by the financial press.

Admittedly, consistently earning 16 percent–plus returns on millions or even billions of dollars takes considerable talent (or some would say, luck). But when you have *thousands* to invest, why play that game when you can do better or just as well with less risk—especially when those returns are tax-free and help the environment? Not even the most celebrated stock jockeys do that.

Most of the investing tips in this section yield at least 16 percent returns—some considerably more. Equally wonderful, they are guaranteed investments that won't induce insomnia or anxiety about when to sell. Sure, many of these recommendations appear to take more effort than calling up your broker with a buy order, but consistently good stock picking requires work, too: investigating products, talking to management, crunching numbers. I'm not suggesting that you ignore the stock market, only that you try these investments first.

1. Shopping for Speculators. Although more and more Americans are hip to the advantages of buying in bulk, case lots, and large quantities when products go on sale, it is still largely an undeveloped and random practice. To hone it to an art, make a list of nonperishables[4] that you use regularly. Include everything from pasta and salsa to dental floss. Don't put anything on the list unless you're sure you really like it. Once you get the case home, mark the date on the box, to see if it gets used enough to justify future large purchases.

Food co-ops or buying clubs give discounts for buying by the case or in quantity. Those co-ops, which use member labor, offer further discounts if you put in a few hours of work.

Unfortunately, co-ops don't always have *the* lowest prices on all items, so if you *must* stretch a budget, it pays to take advantage of sales and specials at supermarkets. You don't need to shop at a superstore regularly to stock up on its loss leaders, which have giveaway prices to lure you in. For some items, like tuna fish, which regularly go on sale, you'll usually save more buying them on sale than placing a case order.

By thinking of smart shopping as investing instead of spending, you won't let a strict budget stop you from taking advantage of good sales. It makes sense to dip into savings to buy $500 worth of groceries when they are 30 percent off—even Warren Buffett would approve. Even if it takes two years to go through all the applesauce you bought, you're still saving 15 percent per year tax free. You've also saved yourself time and trips to the store—as well as partially protected yourself against two years' inflation. Most families can save $50 a month by bulk buying.

---

4. While some hard-core tightwads recommend getting a second freezer for storing bulk frozen foods, I'm skeptical. Unless you use it for serious gardening surplus or are a big meat eater, another freezer won't be worth the extra cost and the additional energy use.

While a family of four living in a one-bedroom apartment may have to pass on bulk buying, think creatively about storage space before deciding it won't work. As tightwad diva Amy Dacyczyn (of *Tightwad Gazette* fame) said, "If you were offered $50 per month to rent out the space under your bed, wouldn't you do it?" There's no reason canned food must kick back in the pantry.

No matter where you live, you can take advantage of buying *services* "in bulk." Whether it is your health club, insurance policy, or a magazine subscription, you often get significant breaks by prepaying multiyear commitments. Heating oil, for example, is usually much cheaper if you preorder a winter's supply before it gets cold.

2. Auto Accounting. Americans spend more on their cars than they do on food, which is bad news for both the environment and our wallets. Cushy retirements could be funded on the money wasted on shiny automobiles and 4 × 4's. (For a full treatment on automobile savings, see "What Your Car *Really* Costs," on page 171.)

To change that scenario, avoid owning a car if you can. If that's not realistic, pay cash for a used, reliable, fuel-efficient model—one *Consumer Reports* approves of. You'll save several ways: First, gas-sippers tend to have lower sticker prices, which means reduced insurance premiums. Second, buying in cash means you avoid blood-letting finance charges. Remember, financing is a profit center for the dealer.

Last, even if gas stays at the subsidized and environmentally harmful price of $1.25 a gallon, good gas mileage pays real dividends. Over the course of 25,000 miles, a car that gets thirty miles per gallon will save $1,041 over a car that gets fifteen per. If you paid $5,000 for your car (remember, I'm recommending used here) and it takes you two years to travel those 25,000 miles, you've earned a 10 percent return from gas savings alone. Add in the savings from insurance and avoided finance charges on a less expensive car and Ivan Boesky will start asking where you get your information.

3. Credit Card Capital. The typical U.S. family owns fourteen credit cards, with a total balance of $5,800. At an average 17 percent yearly interest charge, that's $986 a year in finance fees. Fortunes have been built earning 17 percent interest, so guess what happens when you pay it out? Getting out of debt requires the ol' one-two: one, cut back on any new, optional purchases (that's the environmentally friendly part) to keep your balance from growing; two, use those savings to pay off your debt. If you have any money in a savings account or the market, cash out and pay off Visa first. Why earn 5 percent or even 16 percent and then pay taxes on it when you're sending 17 percent, earned with after-tax dollars, out the door?

While you're whittling down your account, switch your card to one charging lower interest. Many cards charge 8 or 9 percent, at least for an introductory period. Each month *Money* magazine (which is available at any library) lists "the best credit card deals" for those carrying a balance.

If your credit card balance is stubbornly large, consider paying off the debt with a home-equity loan. I offer this cautiously, as defaulting on such a loan could leave you homeless, but the switch does have two advantages. First, the average interest rate on home-equity loans is much lower than that on credit cards. Second, up to $100,000 of home-equity loan interest is tax-deductible. So even if you're in the 28 percent bracket (and itemize), you'll immediately earn a 28 percent return.

4. Fix-It Financing. When you own your own home, invest in some tools and a good how-to book such as the *Reader's Digest Complete Do-It-Yourself Manual.* While not everyone is agile with a hammer and spackling knife, many home improvement projects don't require much skill. And those that do often require expertise for only a small portion of the work. Using hired guns judiciously can really stretch a renovation budget.

Working on your house yourself will make you a smarter homeowner. Even if you ultimately decide it's not for you, you'll know when you need an ace carpenter and when any handyperson will do. You'll also discover that with a $5 snake and five minutes, you'll save $50 when the toilet gets clogged—a 900 percent return on investment.

5. Energy-Audit Earnings. The average American household spends about $1,500 a year on energy. Most homes could reduce that consumption 30 to 40 percent while increasing their comfort. That means many of us are not only polluting more than we have to, we're wasting $450–$600 per year. At guaranteed bank account rates of 5 percent, that's like having an extra $10,000 working for you (except you won't have any taxes to pay on the "income").

Armed with a little knowledge, any homeowner can do a respectable energy audit, checking for air leaks and missing insulation. Caulking and plugging the holes yourself will pay off quickly and earn you a green halo.

But don't stop there: call a house doctor who has a blower

door, smoke pencil, and other thermo-sensitive equipment. The pro will find plenty of leaks you can't yourself. You'll recover the cost of the audit many times over in energy savings—especially as a number of utilities will subsidize the cost. Low utility bills also add equity to your home; buyers are willing to pay more for a home with lower energy costs because they can afford a bigger mortgage.

If you rent, encourage your landlord to have an energy audit. You could offer to implement some of the auditor's recommendations in exchange for rent. Even if you're not responsible for the utility bills, you'll be more comfortable and doing the planet a favor.

6. *Heat Hedging.* For most homes, heating is energy expense numero uno, accounting for two-thirds of yearly energy bills in colder climates. Having an efficient source of heat can make a significant impact on your cash flow and the environment.

Replacing an ancient boiler or furnace is a great investment, often yielding as much as 25 percent per year. Regular maintenance and sometimes replacing outdated burners can also be big winners. If your furnace is only somewhat outdated but functioning, it still can make sense to replace it but requires some quick calculations to see if it makes monetary sense.

When your furnace maintenance person does your regular cleaning (which should be every year for oil units and every two years for gas), ask for the efficiency rating (AFUE) of your existing unit. Also ask if the unit is the proper size for your house, as newer, efficient models can often be smaller and still be effective. The accompanying chart will give you an idea of how much you'll save if you upgrade to a more efficient model, per $100 of fuel you use now.

DOLLAR SAVINGS PER $100 OF ANNUAL FUEL COST

		55%	60%	65%	70%	75%	80%	85%	90%	95%
					AFUE OF NEW SYSTEM					
	50%	$9	$16	$23	$28	$33	$37	$41	$44	$47
	55%		8	15	21	26	31	35	38	42
AFUE	60%			7	14	20	25	29	33	37
OF	65%				7	13	18	23	27	32
EXISTING	70%					6	12	17	22	26
SYSTEM	75%						6	11	16	21
	80%							5	11	16
	85%								5	11

Now you're ready to calculate whether buying a new furnace is a shrewd move. For example, if your existing AFUE is 65 percent and you plan to install a furnace with an AFUE of 95 percent, then your projected savings is $32 per $100. If your annual fuel bill is $1,300, you'll save roughly $416 ($32 × 13) a year. To figure your return on investment, divide that savings (in this case, $416) by the cost of your new furnace—say, $2,800. In this example, that comes to almost 15 percent ($416/$2,800). Riskless, tax-free investing doesn't get much better than that—particularly when you consider the expected life of a heating system *and* the 2.5 tons of carbon dioxide emissions it eliminates each year.

Not all homes and climates require furnaces, of course. Research your options based on your climate, house construction, and individual needs. For moderate and warm climates, for example, heat pumps are often the way to go. And although electric heat tends to be very expensive, its low initial cost can make sense for superinsulated homes or for those in warm climates (it may also be necessary for those with allergies). If you don't mind some sweat equity, woodstoves tend to be the least expensive choice in rural wooded areas. Woodstoves, however, generate considerably more end-source pollution than a boiler—although wood is a renewable resource that doesn't need to be transported from Saudi Arabia.

How you operate your heating system has a big effect on your bills. Even identical houses can have utility bills that vary by 50 percent or more. The savings come from being deft with your thermostat. For each degree that you lower the thermostat, you save about 2 percent on your heating bill. Lower it gradually at first, and over a week or two, your body will comfortably adjust. Most everyone is comfortable at sixty-six to sixty-eight degrees during the day and fifty-five degrees at night. Regularly turning back your thermostat when you leave for work or head to bed will save hundreds of dollars. If you can't seem to remember or hate the idea of waking to a cold house, buy a clock thermostat that can be programmed to kick on just before you wake or return home at night. Your $50 to $150 investment will pay for itself before the first heating season is over.

Turn down the thermostats in unused rooms. Or if you don't have individual controls in each room, lower the main thermostat and spot-heat the room you'll be spending most of your time in. If you have a home office and stay in the one room for hours, having a separate heat source for that room is a fine investment.

7. Cash-Cow Cooling. Most Americans want their homes to be 78 degrees in the winter and 68 in the summer. If only they'd reverse that, our national cooling tab wouldn't come to $25 billion a year, or about $100 per person. In Florida, Arizona, and southern California, it's common for air-conditioning bills to run upward of $500 annually. The good news is, those numbers could easily be reduced by 50 to 75 percent—and with it a similar reduction in the roughly 3,500 pounds of carbon dioxide and 31 pounds of sulfur dioxide each household's cooling energy adds to the atmosphere.

Many strategies similar to those that reduce heating energy costs apply to cooling: adjust the thermostat for an empty house, service and maintain your equipment, and buy the most energy-efficient unit(s) you can. Simple measures such as dressing more lightly in the summer, letting in cool evening air, and acclimatizing to warmer indoor temperatures can make a serious dent in air-conditioning costs.

Your best cooling investments are fans. A good portable fan may rustle loose papers, but it can cool you off at a fraction of the cost of running the AC—and without the ozone-depleting chemicals. A fan offers a return on investment to rival many excellent high-tech stocks.

Whole-house fans, which cost roughly as much as three or four regular fans, draw air from the house up through the attic (which must be ventilated so the hot air escapes). Drawing out the hot air creates cooling breezes and air currents, which lower the temperature throughout the house. Whole-house fans can save 28 to 40 percent on air-conditioning costs.

Recent research indicates favorable results from painting roofs with white, reflective paint. In direct summer heat, dark roofs can reach 180 degrees Fahrenheit (hot enough to fry an egg), and some of the heat from the roof inevitably warms the whole building. Reflective paint can keep 80 percent of the sun's rays from being absorbed. One house tested by the Lawrence Berkley National Laboratory in Sacramento, California, used 40 percent less cooling energy during the summer after roof painting. Before painting the town white, be aware that reflective paint is considerably more expensive than Benjamin Moore's finest and that, as the reflective surface gets dirty over the years, it is likely to lose some of its effectiveness. At this point, it's a good bet for warm climates, but it's too soon to tell if it will be a long-term, blue-chip investment.

8. *Insulation Investing.* Insulation is the backbone of a comfortable, energy-efficient house, keeping the heat in during winter and out during summer. It can also be a darn good investment. Depending upon how much insulation your home already has, and where it is, buttoning up can produce 15 to 40 percent yearly tax-free returns. Adding to scantily clad attic floors and basement ceilings will yield the best returns. Wall insulation payoffs are in the 7 to 15 percent range.

Most people assume they have enough insulation because they noticed some pink stuff in the attic when their real estate agent first showed them around. Upon closer inspection, however, most houses are underinsulated or have gaping holes. In cold regions, for example, only a small percentage of homes have the recommended two feet of insulation above the ceiling. If properly designed, even more insulation than that can do wonders: in frigid parts of Canada and the northern United States, there are superinsulated homes that use only $200 to $300 worth of fuel a year. Even in warmer climates, lots of insulation can produce big savings by eliminating the need for a furnace.

9. Appliance Arbitrage. When buying appliances—especially the biggies, like refrigerators or hot-water heaters—look beyond purchase price to operating cost. That automatic, side-by-side fridge/freezer with ice maker is an energy hog and will ultimately run you a whole lot more than the extra $300 you see on its price tag. By buying an efficient model, you'll save enough in electric bills (compared to the "premium" fridge) to pay for the whole efficient unit in nine years—roughly an 11 percent tax-free return.

Hot-water heaters consume even more energy than refrigerators, costing from $160 to $390 a year (depending upon whether you have electric or gas) to operate. Two no-brainer investments are low-flow shower heads and faucet aerators that save hot water without affecting water pressure. These usually pay for themselves within a few months, providing annual yields of up to 275 percent. Insulating your existing water tank is also a shrewd move, as water heater blankets cost about $10 and can save five times that much in a year— a better percentage return than buying Microsoft at its initial public offering.

Most hot-water heaters are installed by building contractors who profit by using cheap appliances, regardless of their long-term efficiency. If you're stuck with an inefficient electric unit, replace it with an efficient gas one—even if the electric one is still working fine. An efficient gas-powered replacement will often pay for itself in two to three years.

Even more efficient than a gas storage water heater is a

tankless heater that works on demand. These units cost slightly more than the storage variety but can save 20 percent per year in fuel and should last 50 percent longer. If you regularly use a lot of water at once, these units may not be suitable. And before considering one, make sure there is a competent mechanic in your area who can service them; most plumbers still aren't familiar with instantaneous heaters.

Although stand-alone solar-powered water heaters are best for the environment, they don't make good financial investments unless you live in a sunny climate. Solar "batch heaters," however, which prewarm your water before it arrives at your storage tank, can be excellent investments. Batch heaters can pay for themselves in two to five years.

Last, install efficient lighting. Those compact fluorescent bulbs that your utility company has been hawking cost more initially than regular incandescent bulbs, but their energy savings offer a 40 percent return on investment. Fluorescents aren't ideal for every lighting situation but, as a general rule, are worthwhile where you keep lights on for long stretches.

10. Landscape Leverage. Everyone loves a shady tree in the summer and avoids open fields on blustery winter days, but we forget to use these natural principles to create a comfortable, energy-efficient home. Energy-saving landscaping is the most overlooked form of energy conservation there is. Studies show that strategic landscaping can trim heating costs by as much as 30 percent, cut air-conditioning bills by 50 percent, and prune water bills by 40 percent—reaping savings of $300 to $750 a year, depending on the house. The key is to work with nature instead of against it. For example, in cooler climates block northerly winds with trees and bushes and keep your home's southern exposure open.

Besides saving on utility bills, a well-designed landscape can add up to 15 percent to the resale value of your home. And unlike any machine you might invest in, trees and plants never wear out. In fact, they get more valuable as they age.[5]

11. Golden Gardening. Farmer and author Gene Logsdon calculates that, on two-fifths of an acre, the average family of four can grow three-quarters of their food—roughly a $3,000 yearly savings (even more if you normally buy organic). No one claims harvesting that many vegetables is easy. But in addition to saving some gelt, you'll reap other rewards for working in the soil and eating food that hasn't been sprayed with pesticides.

Typical corn and bean gardens are hard to justify on a *financial* basis if you're earning a decent wage, but selective gardening can make bottom-line sense. Stick to expensive, easy-to-grow produce that you really like—such as tomatoes or basil. When organic tomatoes are $3-plus a pound, you can see how just a handful of plants can be worth a couple of hundred dollars of retail value.

TAX YOGA

Start a public discussion about raising or spending tax revenues and watch a brawl. But come April 15, everyone agrees: they want to shake the IRS. With the notable exceptions of Elvis (who liked paying taxes and is one of the largest

5. For details, get a copy of *Energy-Efficient and Environmental Landscaping: Cut Your Utility Bills by Up to 30 Percent and Create a Natural, Healthy Yard* (Appropriate Solutions Press, 953 Dover Road, South Newfane, VT 05351; [802] 348-7441).

taxpayers in U.S. history) and my barber's superpatriot father (who returns his monthly Social Security checks *un*cashed), a convention of happy taxpayers could be held in a powder room. Even those who vote for higher taxes usually want to pay less themselves—if nothing else, so they have more charitable dollars to give away.

Taxes are a drag on savings. To keep from feeling like Sisyphus, you must heed the IRS's power and bend according to its rules. Like a tai chi master, put your energy/money where it flows easiest. Know thy basic tax-saving strategies and learn more about your own particulars.

Although Washington officials are constantly tinkering with the tax code, there are a few tax-savers worth your attention that have remained mostly intact for at least twenty years: tax-deferred retirement plans, municipal bonds, savings from long-term capital gains, and real estate depreciation. No doubt, the particulars governing some of these "shelters" will change again, at least in detail, but given that they have survived numerous congressional tax code battles, they are likely to stick around for a while.

ABOUT FILING

The *second* most annoying thing about taxes—after paying them—is keeping records. To take deductions—and deductions are a major weapon for lowering tax bills—you must be able to document them. If you use your car for business, keep a log of when you use it and save sales slips from gas and repairs (if you take the standard car mileage deduction, you only need to tally the record in your log). Save canceled checks and receipts for a minimum of three years after you file (and if the receipts are connected to the sale of an asset, such as your house or a stock, hold on to them until at least three years after you sell it).

Unless your finances are complicated or you're math-challenged, filing your own 1040 is the best way to save on taxes. Doing it yourself generally isn't very hard (remember, you don't have to know the whole tax code, only what applies to you). There are hordes of books and free IRS services offering help, and you'll benefit from learning what counts as deductions and where they work best—all while avoiding the additional H&R Block levy. If you've got lots of schedules to fill out, can easily afford a CPA, and/or just don't want to deal with it, by all means hire out. Often getting it done professionally one time makes it easy to do it yourself the next year (assuming your tax situation hasn't changed much). Just follow what the accountant did, filling in the blanks with updated numbers yourself.

BUNCHING DEDUCTIONS

One strategy many middle-income filers can use to save taxes and filing hassle is to bunch, as much as possible, two years of itemized deductions into one. Schedule A allows you to deduct mortgage payments, charitable contributions, investment publications and expenses, medical expenditures, local and state taxes, and business-related expenses (if you're self-employed, these go on Schedule C). Since everyone is automatically given a standard deduction, you should only fill out a Schedule A if you go over those amounts.

When your expenses aren't quite up to the standard deduction or are only slightly over, it pays to push as many of those expenses as possible into one year. By prepaying certain bills and taxes from one year, for example, and slightly postponing from another, you'll end up with higher deductions in the year you're targeting—and thus be able to deduct more. Something like an optional medical procedure or charitable contributions (for details on how using a charitable gift fund can work well for this, see pages 252–254) could be timed to maximize their deduction power. Doing this every other year will save you taxes *and* time.

In a similar vein, it sometimes pays to shift when you receive income. Say you know you're going to take a sabbatical next year. Have this year's bonus paid in the following year—when you'll be in a lower bracket. Or if you have your own business, try billing some of this year's sales next year.

TAX-DEFERRED RETIREMENT PLANS

Tax-deferred retirement plans come in two basic flavors: those your employer establishes, such as 401(k) and 403(b), and those you create yourself—IRAs (individual retirement accounts), Keogh plans, and SEPs (simplified employee pension plans), which are primarily designed for the self-employed. There are also two classes of IRAs: regular or the Roth IRA (also known as IRA plus), which can be used regardless of whether you're self-employed or an employee (although there are restrictions for the employed with high incomes). As a general rule, take advantage of retirement plans when you can and start as early as you can (beware: there are penalties for withdrawing before age 59½). Tax-deferred compounding works its magic over time.

Without the bite of taxes, money can grow to astounding

numbers over the long haul. Consider, for example, what happens if, between the ages of twenty and thirty-five, you contribute $1,000 a year to a tax-deferred plan and then do nothing else, but earn 10 percent annual returns. When you withdraw that original $15,000 between the ages of sixty-five and eighty, you'd have $1 million to take out. With 12 percent returns (which is what the stock market has roughly returned since the Depression ended), that hoard would be $3 million. Granted, by that time, after considering inflation, a million dollars won't make you a "real" *millionaire*, but it will be worth a far sight more than the $15,000 it is today.

It's easy to get started. Most large employers have 401(k) and 403(b) "salary-reduction" plans that allow you to shield a certain percentage of your income from taxes. Put aside as much as you can without feeling a tightening in the chest. In many cases, your employer will match your contributions with twenty-five or fifty cents for each dollar you put in. It doesn't take an MBA to recognize that this is a tremendous deal. Take full advantage of it if you can (in this case, put in the highest percentage you're allowed until you feel a tightening in the throat).

Roth IRAs, which were introduced in 1998, add some confusion to the tax-deferred retirement game. What's the difference between a Roth and a regular, deductible-contributions IRA, and which is the better option?[6] Assuming you qualify for both, the major difference is in the tax treatment of the

6. Note that it is also possible to make *non*deductible contributions to a regular IRA, but with the introduction of the Roth IRA, that option no longer makes sense. Nondeductible contributions to a regular IRA have more penalties on early withdrawal and still require you to pay taxes on withdrawals after retiring post–age 59½.

entering and exiting funds. In a regular IRA, contributions are deductible going in and taxed on the way out. Roth IRA contributions aren't deductible, but they can be used penalty free at any time. Gains or investment income earned from those contributions can be withdrawn without taxes or penalties after age 59½ (assuming you've had the Roth IRA for at least five years) or in the case of disability or death, and up to $10,000 can be withdrawn for certain home purchases. Gains used to pay for higher education can be withdrawn penalty free (but not tax free) if you've had the account for more than five years.

Roth IRAs usually make more sense. They give you more flexibility and most times, over the long run, will put more money in your pocket. The exception is if you meet the following conditions: you're less than fifteen years from retirement, you invest your tax savings "earned" from making the deductible contributions, and you'll be in a lower tax bracket when you retire. If you expect to be in the same or a higher bracket after retiring, then the Roth IRA will leave you with more money (as long as you've held it for at least five years).

In addition to IRAs, self-employed folks can set up a Keogh or SEP plan. While the details and restrictions of these plans are available through nearly any bank, the basic gist is, you can shelter substantial amounts of income through these vehicles—up to $30,000 per year.

After funding your retirement plan, there are plenty of investing choices (those options are often more limited through a company plan). If you're a long way off from retirement, stock mutual funds are generally the way to go (see the recommendations in the "Investing" chapter). A fund's diversity greatly increases your chances of getting good returns—as long as you hold, hold, hold, riding out market dips. Owning a stock fund in your retirement account also eliminates one of the hassles of mutual funds: having to report yearly capital gains and dividend distributions—an expense and a filing annoyance come tax time.

If you insist on buying individual stocks in your IRA or 401(k), make sure you research them carefully and stick to well-established companies. Losers in a retirement account don't even get the benefit of a tax write-off. Highfliers and tips from the boss's accountant may be fun once in a while, just don't do it in your retirement account.

It should go without saying that you should *not* buy already tax-advantaged investments such as municipal bonds in your retirement account, but I am saying it anyhow because, as a broker, I saw such mistakes on numerous occasions.

TAX-ADVANTAGED INVESTMENTS

BUYING TAX-FREE BONDS

The interest from debt issued from states, municipalities, and their various agencies is free from federal taxes. That interest is also exempt from state and local taxes if it comes from a bond issued from your state (or from Puerto Rico or other U.S. territories).

Why doesn't everyone buy muni bonds or tax-free mutual funds? Mostly because they pay a lower interest rate than taxable bonds and therefore only make sense for those in the 28 percent tax bracket and higher. If you don't know what tax bracket you're in—that is, how much tax you pay on your last dollar of income—figure it out from the tax charts the

IRS includes in its tax forms. There is a simple formula to determine whether tax-free bonds make more sense than taxable ones:

1. Subtract your tax bracket from 1. For example:
$$1 - .31 \text{ (a 31\% bracket)} = .69$$
2. Then divide that fraction of 1 (in this case, .69) by the taxable yield to find the tax-free equivalent. For example:
$$7\% \div .69 = 10.14\%$$

In other words, a 7 percent tax-free yield is the same as getting 10.14 percent from taxable bonds.

(For more details about municipal bonds and their socially responsible possibilities, see pages 86–87.)

BUYING AND HOLDING STOCKS

Investing oracle Warren Buffett has become one of America's richest citizens in two ways: by picking great stocks and, equally important, by giving back very little to the tax lady. With a net worth north of $20 billion, Buffett has only paid roughly $30 million in taxes. He hasn't managed this by employing fast-fingered accountants or finding a tax haven off the coast of South America; Buffett simply doesn't sell his investments that perform well. By buying winners and letting them ride, his ever-increasing hoard freely compounds. Taxes aren't due until he takes profits.

Of course, you and I won't pick stocks as well as Buffett does, but the basic strategy of holding winning stocks is a good one—and requires less work than trying to find the latest hot pick. Most investors are reverse trigger-happy. When they have a winner, they quickly lock in profits, and when their picks head south, they continue to hold (in denial that "the market" just may know more than they do).

For most nonprofessionals, it's better to set a limit on losses (pay especially close attention when the overall stock market is doing well but your company is dragging or falling) and use those as deductions come tax time: losses can offset gains or count against income up to $3,000 a year. Beyond that you must carry the loss forward to future years.

By letting your winners ride, you pay less in commissions and less taxes. Long-term gains (held more than eighteen months) are taxed at the maximum of 20 percent (no, that doesn't benefit those in the 15 percent bracket). And after 2001, the maximum rate will be 18 percent if an asset is held more than five years. Holding winners is also more relaxing: it not only takes less research, but once you're sitting on a large gain, when price gyrations do come, they're less worrisome (giving back some gains doesn't hurt as much as turning into a net loser).

BUYING REAL ESTATE

Buying real estate you manage yourself isn't exactly a holistic investment since it can be a lot of work—as much a part-time job as an investment. You need to know local property values, be good at negotiating and managing rentals, and be prepared for late-night phone calls complaining about a failed furnace or leaky ceiling. If you can live with those inconveniences, then real estate does have much to recommend it: good returns, tax advantages, and the possibility of being a humane, environmentally sensitive landlord.

The tax benefits from real estate come from depreciation and a favorable capital gains rate when you sell. The tax code insists that you depreciate rental property over 27.5 years—even if it is actually appreciating. So say you purchase a small apartment building for $275,000 that produces a net income after expenses of $10,000 a year. You wouldn't have to pay taxes on that income because you'd get to deduct $10,000 ($\frac{1}{27.5}$ of $275,000) a year in depreciation.

That $10,000 depreciation deduction reduces the cost basis of your property each year. So if you were to hold the property for 27.5 years, from the IRS's point of view, you got the building for nothing. If you sold the property for the same $275,000 you paid for it, you'd still owe taxes on a $275,000 "gain." Sounds like a bum deal, until you consider two things: First, the $275,000 gain is considered long-term so it gets favorable tax treatment; long-term gains resulting from depreciation are taxed at a maximum rate of 25 percent, and gains from genuine appreciation pay no more than 20 percent in taxes (after 2001, the five-year/18 percent max will kick in). Essentially, you've deferred paying the taxes you "owe" on the rental income until when you sell the property—and then you pay at a rate that is likely to be lower than your normal one.

Second, of course, you don't have to sell. You could just keep collecting rent. Or assuming you've paid the mortgage down or the building has appreciated (or both), you could take out a loan against the building's equity—basically taking out most of the worth of the building—without owing any taxes on that money.

ENJOY THE TAX BENEFITS OF HOME OWNERSHIP

Homeowners get tax benefits from itemizing mortgage costs and when they sell their property for a profit. A couple can make up to $500,000 on a primary residence tax free ($250,000 for singles and couples filing separately). Since this extravagant tax break can be recycled every two years, you could buy a fixer-upper, live in it and make repairing it your full-time job, and then sell it—essentially making your income from the repair work tax-free (assuming you sold it at a gain).

INVESTING

WHERE TO PUT YOUR INVESTMENT DOLLARS

Financial advisers typically use a pyramid to illustrate how we should allocate our assets. At the base, the old saw goes, should be cash, your home, insurance, bank CDs, and bonds. The middle section, where the pyramid narrows, represents your riskier investments, which have the potential for higher returns—such as stocks or investment real estate. And at the tippy-top—that is, with the smallest portion of your money—it's suggested you foray into the most speculative of investments: things like options, commodities, microstocks, and raw land.

It's true that establishing a solid financial foundation is important: make sure you're out of debt, have emergency cash set aside, are properly insured, and (when appropriate) own your home—which is energy-efficient and stocked with appropriate bulk purchases. But the pyramid model has its limits.

For starters, no matter how much gelt you have, there's no reason to invest in undeveloped land or play the most dangerous games, such as commodities and options. These are losing games, except for professionals or wily veterans (and the brokerage houses that came up with the pyramid model in the first place). High-stakes speculating also tends to become obsessive. For those who enjoy the thrill, can afford to take losses, and can keep a lid on the greed and gambling itch, then have some fun. But you're not missing out if you stick to basic investments with less razzmatazz.

More important than forming a pyramid is heeding the intersection of your age, assets, investing time horizon, and— just as important—comfort with risk. It's quite possible and reasonable that, after taking care of basic financial responsibilities, you will have more money in the "risky section" than your supposedly larger "safe foundation" (forming an upside-down trapezoid shape). Or despite pep talks about the upward-trending stock market, you decide to stay largely on the sidelines. The pain of watching your savings disappear may simply outweigh the pleasure of seeing them multiply. Surviving long-term downturns is easy on paper, but enduring ten or even fifteen years when your retirement account looks more like a sieve than a silo is another matter. One investing adage that still rings true is: Sell down to your sleeping point.

The accompanying table (on page 83) gives simple guidelines for allocating your investments, assuming you have a long-term investing horizon (ideally of ten-plus years, but no less than five) *and* you've already taken care of your financial essentials. Funds earmarked for a house, business, or tuition payments scheduled within a few years should be in investments that guarantee principal (or close to it).

Investing in rental property hasn't been included in the allocation chart because that usually takes more effort and know-how than investing in the stock and bond markets (as well as more funds). But if you know what you're doing and have the inspiration, time, and cash to invest in rental property, by all means do so. You'll have more control over the effect of your investment than with stocks and bonds and have a hedge against inflation with tax benefits to boot. If that's the route you go, feel free to switch most or part of your stock allocation to real estate.

If you don't want to be a landlord, a much easier way to protect your investments against inflation is to buy a commodity index fund. Not to be confused with commodity hedge funds—which tend to crash or occasionally zoom based on the manager's speculative prowess—an index fund matches the price changes of basic commodities. Until recently, outside of real estate, the only way to hedge against inflation was speculating in lumber futures, storing Krugerrands in your safe-deposit box, or investing in a commodity index overseas. Now it's as simple as filling out a form and sending a check to a mutual fund company. When the cost of raw materials increases, so does the index's value. Since stock and bond values tend to move opposite to inflation—at least in the short run—a commodity index fund can lower the volatility of (and thus your worry about) your investments. A 5 to 10 percent allotment is appropriate. If even this "simplified" commodity index option sounds too complicated, don't sweat it—you can stick to more standard investments instead, especially if you remain truly calm when your portfolio dips. (Don't forget that long-term outlook.)

RECOMMENDED ALLOCATION OF LONG-TERM ASSETS

INVESTING ATTITUDE	PERCENTAGE IN FIXED INCOME	PERCENTAGE IN STOCKS
NEGATIVE NUMBERS MAKE YOU SWEAT	= YOUR AGE + 30	= 70 - YOUR AGE
LIKE SAFETY	= YOUR AGE	= 100 - YOUR AGE
MODERATE	= YOUR AGE - 10	= 110 - YOUR AGE
AGGRESSIVE	= YOUR AGE - 20	= 120 - YOUR AGE
BUDDHA-LIKE UNFLAPPABILITY IN BEAR MARKETS	= YOUR AGE - 45	= 145 - YOUR AGE

NOTES: FIXED INCOME INCLUDES CDS, BONDS, AND OTHER RELATED INVESTMENTS SUCH AS GOVERNMENT NATIONAL MORTGAGE ASSOCIATION (GNMA) FUNDS; STOCKS CAN ALSO MEAN MUTUAL FUNDS—OR AS NOTED IN THE TEXT, INVESTMENT REAL ESTATE.

ANYTHING OVER 100 PERCENT—I.E., IF YOU'RE YOUNGER THAN 45 IN THE LAST CATEGORY—MEANS THAT EVERYTHING WOULD BE IN "STOCKS."

Remember, the profiles given in the table are guidelines, not straitjackets. Try one on and see if it fits. If you're not sure which to do first, try the "moderate" and then adjust. If I had to choose the definitive holistic mix, it would be 65 percent stocks and 35 percent bonds/fixed income. Under that scenario, from 1970 to 1996 (a period that included a mean bear and a raging bull market), you would have averaged almost 11.5 percent annual returns—only .7 percent lower yearly returns than an all-stock portfolio but with considerably less volatility (and thus angst).

To mirror this stock-bond mix with one-stop investing shopping (for those not in high tax brackets), there is a socially responsible mutual fund (a professionally managed portfolio) called Pax World, which invests 70 percent in stocks and 30 percent in bonds. It is the oldest of all socially responsible investing (SRI) funds and has been a steady, solid performer, averaging 12 percent returns over the last twenty years.

Remember, make no correlation between investing style and lifestyle, attitudes, or moral fiber. Conservative and aggressive investors come in all political and social stripes. There's no right or wrong way to feel about risking your money.

FIXED-INCOME INVESTMENTS

Fixed-income vehicles offer a reliable, stable source of income. To understand how they work, it's best to look at bonds, the original of the genre. Bonds are basically IOUs issued by corporations, municipalities, governments, and their agencies. The terms of that IOU—namely, when the bond comes due and the interest rate it pays—determine how much the borrower must fork over.

If a bond matures soon, it tends to pay a low rate, similar to a money market. The yield on longer-term bonds is affected by the general interest rate climate and the bond issuer's creditworthiness—an MBA's way of saying, "How likely is the borrower to make good on the payments?" The ability to deliver the goods is rated by outside agencies such as Moody's or Standard & Poor's. Not surprisingly, financially shaky borrowers must pay investors higher yields.

The trickiest concept for most new bond investors to understand is the inverse relationship between bond prices and interest rates. That is, when rates rise, bond prices fall, and when rates drop, prices climb.

To see how this works, consider a $1,000 bond that pays a 10 percent coupon rate (or $100 per year) and matures in ten years. Should interest rates shoot up overnight or the bond issuer's creditworthiness plummet, the ten-year bond may need to pay 13 percent to attract investors. In that case, the bond would be worth $770 if you tried to sell it ($100/$770 = 13 percent) or wanted to buy more.[1]

Such sudden, drastic price changes are unusual; price fluctuations tend to be milder than that, especially for short- and medium-term bonds. If the increase in interest rates had happened very gradually, over the decade, the price dip wouldn't be significant since bonds trade near their face value as their maturity date approaches. And regardless of where rates are when the bond comes due, you'd get your original $1,000 principal back. Should the bond issuer declare bankruptcy, you probably would be burned for most of your investment, but bondholders at least stand ahead of stockholders to collect from the sale of assets.

Of course, interest rates could also fall; then your bonds would be worth more. The only potential snafu in this scenario is that many bonds come with a *call provision*. That is, the bond issuer has the right to recall its bonds before maturity (often at only a slight premium). Obviously, the issuer would only do that when it can refinance at a significantly lower rate. If that happens, though, you'd unfortunately only be able to reinvest at a lower rate, too. Ask about a bond's call provision before buying.

The reason to own bonds is their simplicity, certainty of

1. For simplicity's sake, at the moment I'm ignoring the difference between the bid and the ask price—that is, the gap (usually a small one) between what the highest buyer is willing to pay and the lowest seller is offering. Every investor loses a little when he or she buys at the ask and sells at the bid (plus commissions).

income, and lower volatility—as bond prices tend to fluctuate considerably less than stocks. For social investors, bonds also offer opportunities to support worthwhile projects.

The bad news about bonds is, they don't provide growth. Historically, returns from bonds have barely kept ahead of inflation, and when taxes are taken into consideration, you sometimes come out a net loser. Only in a deflationary, depression-type financial climate will safe bonds outperform stocks for many years.

THE MENU AND HOUSE RECOMMENDATIONS

Bonds come in a wide variety of flavors, and when you add in other, similar fixed-income investments—such as bank certificates of deposit, bond mutual funds, mortgage-backed securities, convertibles, and unit trusts—it can send a head spinning. Thankfully, you don't need to mess with all of them. A limited menu will work just fine.

The first major choice to make is, taxable or tax-free?

TAX-FREE BONDS

Tax-free bonds are municipal bonds issued by states, counties, or cities and their various agencies. All other bonds are taxable. Since munis pay less than their taxable brethren, don't even consider the tax-free domain unless you're in the 28 percent federal tax bracket or above. Also note that tax-free bonds are sold in minimum lots of $5,000, although bond mutual funds are available for less. Here's a simple formula for comparing tax-free and taxable yields to see which puts more money in your pocket after you tithe to Uncle

Sam (this formula is illustrated with an example on page 76, in the "Tax-Advantaged Investments" subsection):

$$\text{tax equivalent yield} = \text{muni bond yield}/(1 - \text{your tax rate})^2$$

Most municipal bonds of various stripes and sizes are kosher for socially conscious investors. There are exceptions, like revenue bonds raising money for an incinerator, wetlands-trashing real estate development, or the rare nuke-funding bond, such as the infamous, bankrupt WPPSS bonds (universally called "whoops," but officially the Washington Public Power Supply System). But for the most part, obviously cities and states use their money for civic purposes. At least you needn't worry about the state of Rhode Island buying missiles and funding the CIA with the proceeds from its bond issue.

Some socially conscious investors like knowing exactly what their investments are funding and seek out bonds issued for projects they like—such as funding hospital or school construction, funding housing projects for the elderly, rehabilitating a decaying urban area, or funding a recycling program. Such bonds aren't always available, especially if you live in a small or less populated state. You may need to be patient (ask your broker about the upcoming muni offering calendar) or buy out-of-state bonds. The downside to out-of-state bonds is, their interest isn't free from your state and local income taxes (as mentioned earlier in this subsection, only bonds issued in your own state or a U.S. territory such as Puerto Rico are totally tax-free).

---

2. Include your state and local taxes in your tax rate if you are buying bonds issued in your state or from Puerto Rico or other U.S. territories.

TAXABLE BONDS

Although they aren't very exotic, bank certificates of deposit (CDs) are the best choice for those who are not in the higher tax brackets. Socially responsible banks and credit unions (see pages 45–48 for more about choosing one), which make loans to progressive or worthwhile enterprises, come with a government guarantee, and their CDs are easy to buy. CD yields usually beat U.S. Treasury bonds (which are free from local taxes), even after you pay state and city income tax. Almost every bank and credit union has CDs with maturities of at least five years, and some offer seven-year CDs.

For taxable fixed-income investment beyond seven years, the easiest, highest-yielding, and most liquid choice is a Ginnie Mae mutual fund. Ginnie Maes are pools of mortgage-backed securities backed by federal housing agencies such as the Federal Housing Administration (FHA) and Department of Veterans Affairs and issued by the Government National Mortgage Association (GNMA). In plain English, that means your money will help house people and your investment is very safe. Ginnie Maes pay well, too, often one or as much as two percentage points higher than Treasury bonds.

Don't try to handle Ginnie Mae on your own: she's expensive (issued in $25,000 minimums) and a complex gal since Ginnie Maes pay back both interest and principal and can be prepaid unpredictably (as you'd expect with mortgages). Buying Ginnie Maes through a mutual fund eliminates all that messiness. By pooling your money with that of other investors and having a professional manager buy the Ginnie Maes, a fund allows you to buy in small increments, and you can reinvest your income or take it without principal. When considering a Ginnie Mae fund, look for one with a low expense ratio (listed near the front of the prospectus or noted in fund newsletters such as *Morningstar*, which is available in most libraries).

A simple, long-term bond alternative to GNMA funds, which will pay less current interest but have greater price appreciation when rates drop, is U.S. Treasury bonds. They are safe, simple to understand, and easy to buy and sell. Since you may feel uncomfortable underwriting all of Uncle Sam's payroll, consider buying U.S. government agency bonds. Most socially conscious investors feel comfortable buying bonds issued by the Federal Housing Administration, Bank for Cooperatives, Federal Farm Credit System, Small Business Administration, and Postal Service. These bonds usually carry the same federal guarantee against default that Treasury securities do—and even those agency bonds that don't come with official guarantees have the implicit expectation that the government stands behind them. Most funding for federal agencies is done through the Federal Financing Bank, which also offers its own bond issues.

HOW TO BUY BONDS WITHOUT FEARING INFLATION

Inflation is a bond's worst enemy; deflation, its best friend. Since interest rates rise during inflationary times, the price of bonds drops (remember that inverse relationship).

If you're buying individual bonds or CDs, the best way to protect yourself is to create a bond ladder—each rung of the ladder consisting of a differently maturing bond. For CDs and taxable investments, this can be done with as little as $5,000 or $10,000. For municipal bonds it will take at least $25,000 and ideally $50,000-plus, since munis sell in $5,000 denominations.

A classic laddered portfolio would consist of bonds with maturities of one year, two years, three years, right up to ten years. (For taxable investors it would be CDs up to seven years and then long-term government bonds or a GNMA fund.) After you set this up, each time a bond comes due, you buy another ten-year bond (at which point the two-year bond would then be a one-year bond). Bond yields tend to flatten out around ten years, meaning you usually get roughly the same yield with ten-year bonds as with twenty- or thirty-year paper. And should you need the cash before maturity, the prices of ten-year bonds fluctuate considerably less than long-term ones—even if rates have gone up.

If the once-a-year adjusting it takes to maintain such a ladder is more than you care to mess with, or if you don't have a large amount to invest, spread the rungs two years apart.

When you can buy bonds regularly (as opposed to having one large lump sum to invest), buy the longer-term maturities each time, and eventually this will create a ladderesque situation (even if it doesn't have perfectly spaced rungs).

WHY INVEST IN STOCKS? AND AN EASY, WINNING STRATEGY

The stock market can be a frustrating and anxious place—even during bull markets. Fluctuating prices toy with our hot-buttons of greed and fear, breeding irrational optimism or panic. A bad earnings report, the threat of a U.S.-Japanese trade war, or a car skidding into the Federal Reserve Board chairman can send your life savings into a tailspin. Hardly sounds like the stuff of holistic personal finance. Why mess with it, you ask?

Basically for the same bold-faced reason Willie Sutton liked banks: it's where the money is. Stocks have proved to be the best-returning investment vehicle ever invented. Fortunes can be built from small investments, and with just a little know-how and lots of patience, you can almost predictably grow rich. Owning a piece of public companies is your best chance for your savings to stay ahead of inflation and taxes. And as a shareholder, you get a voice—a chance to influence how corporations behave.

The payoff from investing in stocks over the long haul has been widely touted (even within these pages). And while that song tends to be sung the loudest toward the end of bull markets, the facts speak for themselves: since 1926, stocks have averaged returns of 10 to 12 percent per year, leaving Treasury bonds (at 5 percent) and bank interest (at 3 percent) in the dust. Going back to 1802, when the stock market and capitalism as we know it were toddlers, a single dollar invested in the market would have been worth $2,755,000 in 1998, a return of about 8 percent a year. After taxes and inflation, that dollar would still have grown to $83,700. The same buck invested in "safe" long-term government bonds would have netted $230.

That said, there is good reason to tread carefully: on any given day, the market is almost as likely to go down as up—and there have been some dismal five- and ten-year stretches, when owning stocks was about as much fun as receiving treatments from a fumbling acupuncturist.

But when you have a long-term investing horizon, the bad

times are more the exception than the rule. There is little to fear if history even vaguely repeats itself. A composite of New York Stock Exchange company stocks purchased on any day of its history would always have made a profit over any fifteen-year period—and over any twenty-year period, stocks topped bonds and savings accounts.

While investing for the long run sounds easy—after all, you just let it sit there—the reality of holding stocks through a severe market downturn can be gut-wrenching. Waiting for all the king's men, after watching your nest egg fall and leak, requires a deep faith in long-term investing or genuine non-attachment to money. It's easier to cultivate both if you don't need the funds anytime soon. How do I define *soon*? Within five years at the least, although it's even better if you have a ten-year-plus horizon.

The good news is, outside of being patient, there's little else you must know to do well in the stock market. *The Wall Street Journal* regularly holds a contest pitting the stock picks of the country's top money managers (the professionals who choose stocks for mutual funds and other institutions) against its own random selections—chosen literally by throwing darts against the financial pages while blindfolded. It's usually a toss-up as to who wins.

The stock-picking game is so competitive that, for most investors, chasing hot stocks and mutual funds is a waste of time—and often costly. For most investors, the way to go is to buy an index fund, which invests in companies on a predetermined roster, based on their size and/or socially conscious bill of health. Since index funds are passively run, they charge lower management fees and trade much less than other mutual funds. They aren't subject to the emotional mistakes even the "pros" make.

Index funds usually outperform 80 percent of all fund managers and leave more money in your pocket—with less paperwork. Most funds generate yearly capital gains distributions, which require you to pay taxes (unless the fund is held in a tax-deferred retirement account) even if you haven't sold your shares. Since indexes sell much less than the typical fund, they create fewer capital gains distributions.

Of course, some fund managers do consistently beat the market indexes—at least for a while. And this keeps hordes of fund junkies hunting for *the* manager. In the last fifteen to twenty years, there has been an explosion in new mutual funds, accompanied by a boom in magazines, newsletters, television shows, and Web sites devoted to their tracking, evaluating, and forecasting. This glut of financial product and information has turned what was supposed to be an easy investment vehicle into a potentially very complicated selection process.

Don't sweat the tracking game: it's hardly worth the effort. Those fund managers who do shine usually find that either their luck runs out or they're flooded with money. Either way, you've missed the gravy train: the fund closes to new investors, or the incoming billions make it difficult for the manager to invest in smaller companies without inflating the stock's price. And it's small companies that are most likely to offer unrecognized values. The only companies they can buy are among the very biggest—which are usually the ones that everyone else is buying and scrutinizing so closely—effectively putting a bullet in their outstanding-results legs.

Rather than play the performance derby, stick with an index fund and do dollar cost averaging (discussed later in this chapter). If the average fund sleuth traded his research time (and financial publication subscription fees) for overtime at work or making his home energy-efficient—and then put that extra cash into an index fund—he'd have more money with far less bother.

With virtually no investing effort, indexing gives the smug satisfaction of knowing that your portfolio is outperforming the vast majority of trust departments, investment advisers, mutual fund managers, and private investors who are busy scheming away.

SO WHAT'S THE BEST MUTUAL FUND?

Unfortunately, there isn't a simple, the-envelope-please answer to what's *the* best mutual fund. While I obviously like index funds for their simplicity and excellent returns, they aren't necessarily the best choice for the risk-sensitive.

Still, consider index funds first since they are likely to give the best performance in the long run. Socially conscious investors have only a few index funds to choose from. The main alternatives are the Domini Social Equity Fund and the Citizens Trust Index. They're pretty similar: both are no-load (i.e., no up-front sales charge), socially screened, and pared-down takeoffs of the stock market bellwether, the Standard & Poor's 500; they hold roughly two hundred of the same stocks in their portfolios (out of a 400 total for Domini and a 300 total for Citizens); both have, on average, outperformed the S&P 500 by about 1 percent a year, annually earning *Morningstar*'s coveted 5-star rating; and both pursue shareholder resolutions to improve corporate behavior (see pages 106–115 for why that's important).

There are, however, some subtle differences between Domini and Citizens: namely, in social screens and performance. Citizens Trust is more focused on environmentally benign companies and is a bit stricter in whom it will allow in its index. For example, it has no oil stocks in its portfolio and it will even drop SRI darlings like Merck for environmental transgressions. In 1998 Franklin Research, an independent SRI-fund watchdog, recognized the slightly stricter standards of Citizens by giving it an A− for its social, nonfinancial standards; Domini received a B+. (No fund received an A or A+.) Domini, however, has filed more shareholder resolutions than Citizens.

As a result of its ecofilters, Citizens Trust holds more technology-based businesses and less heavy-industry companies than Domini. The downside to this is Citizens Trust tends to be a tad more volatile than Domini; the upside is that in strong markets Citizens Trust has performed a wee bit better. Over the long run, however, Domini is likely to give slightly better returns simply because it charges lower fees (Domini deducts .98 percent a year from shareholders versus 1.59 percent per annum for Citizens Index). Domini is also likely to put more money in your after-tax pocket since it makes fewer changes in its holdings. During 1998, for instance, Domini's portfolio turnover was just 1 percent; Citizens' was 19 percent—still a good number compared to most funds (many of which go over 100 percent per year), but it means that a Citizens shareholder will probably have more tax-related paperwork to handle. (This is a nonissue if you're holding the fund in a retirement account.)

For those who prefer investing in an index fund that benefits nonprofits, consider the Green Century Equity Fund and DEVCAP. The Green Century fund is run by a consortium of environmental-advocacy groups, and DEVCAP contributes a portion of shareholder profits to organizations that fund microenterprise loans in developing countries. Both funds invest shareholders' money in the Domini Index, which means they must charge higher fees than Domini does (1.5 percent for Green Century and 2 percent for DEVCAP).

If you're sensitive to market fluctuations and content to trade in the juiciest bottom line for peace of mind, consider two nonindex, no-load funds: Ariel Appreciation and Pax World Balanced. Ariel Appreciation's returns haven't quite kept pace with Domini and Citizens, but they've still been impressive, given the fund has been roughly one-third less volatile than the indexes. Note, however, that Ariel Appreciation, while strict in its stock screening, is less vigorous in its shareholder activism than the other funds mentioned here.

Pax World, ballasted by 30 percent of its portfolio in bonds, is even less volatile than Ariel Appreciation. Naturally Pax World won't keep pace with Domini, Citizens, or Ariel in bull markets, but in down markets Pax World tends to sell off by only half as much as the benchmarks. Pax World compares well with any balanced fund (the category of funds that hold both stocks and bonds): it often shows up at the top of the charts ranking *all* balanced funds in yearly and quarterly reviews and historically trounces other SRI balanced funds.

As noted in "Where to Put Your Investment Dollars," Pax World's mix of stocks and bonds offers those in lower tax brackets the pleasing simplicity of a single investment vehicle for relatively calm and consistent growth. Pax World screens both its stocks and bonds—refusing to own government bonds that could fund military spending. As with any *nonindex* fund (this holds for Ariel Appreciation, too, of course), before investing be sure to check the fund's prospectus and the latest, independent appraisal (by *Morningstar*, for example) to see if there have been any management changes since this writing.

If you can't resist trying to beat the index averages or you need outstanding returns to, say, stretch your college fund, you must venture outside the strictly SRI-marketed universe. Consider a health-care-sector fund or, as a distant second choice, a technology fund. None of these do shareholder activism or even stock screening per se, but these sectors are gentler than most industries, even holding less objectionable stocks than some SRI funds. (Since some tech companies have military contracts, many social investors consider them off-limits. But there are plenty of companies that don't—or as only a tiny percentage of revenues—and high-tech companies tend to have progressive employee policies and pollute less than traditional manufacturers or conglomerates. Read the prospectus to see if a fund's holdings are offensive.)

Health-care and technology stocks have outperformed the overall market over the last ten years, and if futurists are even half-right, both these areas promise big growth well into the 2000s. Health-care stocks have actually been less volatile than the overall market, but be prepared to rock and roll with technology funds, which can occasionally free-fall as well as soar.

DOLLAR COST AVERAGING: A SIMPLE, SAFE, AND PROFITABLE WAY TO INVEST IN MUTUAL FUNDS

Dollar cost averaging is investor-speak for consistent investing in either mutual funds or stocks (although for most investors it's recommended only for a fund). Rather than plunging headlong into the market, dollar cost averaging lets you get wet a little at a time. The idea is to invest regularly so you buy more shares when the market dips and fewer when it is "expensive"—a strategy that beats the performance of 99 percent of the self-proclaimed market-timing wizards.

Here's an example of how it works: Let's say you invest $200 each month. The first month you buy ten shares of a $20 fund. A dramatic sell-off drops your fund to $10 a share. Assuming it stayed at the $10 price for five months and you keep investing, it would only take a price recovery of $11.66 for you to break even.

This reduces the fear of price drops. In fact, when you have a long-term view, you welcome market dips because they offer a chance to load up at lower prices, knowing that eventually the market will come back. Of course, this method would stink if your shares never recovered, so don't do it for individual stocks unless you have the utmost confidence in their long-term prospects. Historically, broad-based funds always bounce back and then some.

Part of the appeal of dollar cost averaging is its simplicity. After choosing a fund, just regularly buy it or have purchases automatically deducted from your bank account. The only bit of complication comes at tax-reckoning time when you sell your fund. Over the years dollar cost averagers will develop a myriad of cost-of-purchase prices for their fund. When you cash out, you need to know your original cost basis of those shares (save your statements until you sell). You also must designate which shares you are selling—that is, recently acquired or "old" shares (sell the highest-priced ones first, unless you have losses to offset gains).

This bookkeeping hassle can be reduced by investing either every quarter, semiannually, or even annually—although some investing hawks will point out that doing it annually means losing out on a whole year of earning stock market returns.

When you have a large lump-sum investment to make, statistics show that in the *long run* you get the best returns by putting the full sum into the market right away—even if you buy at high tide in a market cycle. What these stats ignore is an investor's peace of mind. Splitting a large total into smaller pieces, then investing it gradually will make your savings less susceptible to sharp downturns. Consider setting up a five-year bond ladder (see "How to Buy Bonds without Fearing Inflation," earlier in the chapter) and investing funds into the market when a bond comes due.

FOR THOSE WHO WANT TO MAKE THEIR OWN PICKS

Most investors should stick with mutual funds. Choosing your own stocks can be time-consuming and usually produces worse results than if you had stuck with a fund. Do-it-yourselfers often make expensive mistakes, not realizing what they don't know. *Homo economicus* has a tendency to agonize over big winners he thought about buying but didn't, while forgetting about the dead balloons he had also passed on. Then, unaware that picking and staying with most winners is much harder when actual dollars are on the line, the novice dives in—so often at high tide, only to sell at the low.

That said, those who learn to swim, knowing when to stay calm, when to go against the currents, and when to ride the waves—and most important, enjoy the sport—will find they have some advantages over fund managers and thus fund investors.

Buying your own stocks gives you more control over the kind of companies you buy and a chance to have your voice heard by management. If you don't want McDonald's in your portfolio, you don't have to have it—even if a fund manager/social screen thinks the company is swell for donating millions to charity.

A savvy individual investor even has a performance edge over a big fund. The fiduciary responsibilities, legal restrictions, and size of most mutual funds handcuff investment managers. Mutual fund managers, for example, must contend with quarterly performance pressures that individuals don't. To look good before a report comes out, managers often buy the stock du jour—even if they don't think the timing is right.

A small investor can move nimbly in and out of any stock. She can hold a handful or two of great companies instead of trying to find dozens of them (the average fund owns 120 stocks). She can also control the timing of when she sells, which—when you own good stocks—has the advantage of letting your winners run, compounding returns without taxes taking a cut. And last, but definitely not least, flying solo avoids paying annual fund costs, which include management fees (sometimes more than 2 percent a year), *plus* operating costs, and possibly a sales load (which is a one-time charge).

STOCK-PICKING GUIDELINES

While the art of stock picking—and it is more art than science—can get complex and theoretical, in its essence it's fairly simple. A stockholder is a part owner of a company; when you buy shares, your fortune is hitched to the company's. Any change in the corporation's worth affects your slice of it. The best investors evaluate a business's value and forecast its future better than anyone else.

Of course, accurately assessing a company's value and foreseeing its prospects does take some skill and know-how. But the most important tools are common sense, a willingness to research, and discipline. About all the math you need you learned by junior high.

There are three basic reasons your company will increase in value: First, stocks in general go up. Typically, this happens when interest rates are either dropping or expected to fall; then the returns that stocks offer look better than alternative investments—such as bonds or money markets.

Second, you invest in a company whose assets hadn't previously been recognized. Railroad stocks, for example, shot up a few years ago when investors realized that these companies were sitting on loads of valuable real estate. If someone bought the company outright and sold its land, he or she would get more than the stock's value (share price × the number of shares outstanding).

Third, you own a company whose sales and earnings are growing—or are expected to. Fast-growing companies are easy to find. The hard part is finding ones everyone else doesn't already know about. Most companies with a bright future have already been discovered by the investment community. Their stock price reflects that rosy outlook. If blossoming earnings don't come to pass, or not as quickly as eager investors demand, the stock's price (again, read company's value) will fall or stall.

Part-time investors should concentrate on the third area: buying companies that are likely to have increasing sales and earnings. Trying to find companies with undiscovered hidden assets requires lots of research. And predicting the short-term direction of stocks has proved to be a holy grail that few—if any—have mastered.

Small forests have been cleared for books that explain how to invest in profitable, growing companies. And before flying solo, you're advised to read some (for an accessible introduction, read Peter Lynch's *One Up on Wall Street*). No matter how you slice it, if you want to play the stock game, you need to know some numbers; numbers are, after all, the language of business.

To get a grasp on how a company is doing and valued, you should understand what is meant by things like price/earnings (P/E) ratio, earnings growth rate, inventory levels, and return on equity. But once you know the basics, don't get carried away—unless you want to quit your day job. Many stock-picking methods, while effective for good returns, require a great deal of research and tinkering. By noting the guidelines presented here, it is possible to make stock picking a simpler, less stressful, and profitable affair. The idea is to have your stocks work for you, not the other way around. Use the following guidelines to temper what you learn elsewhere (see appendix for book recommendations):

Invest in Companies You Understand. You don't need to know biochemistry to invest in a pharmaceutical company, but you should have a good sense of the company's products and services and why they're better than the competition's. It's much easier to tell how Ben & Jerry's will do as a company after you taste its newest low-fat flavors than to evaluate Caterpillar when you don't know a backhoe from a front-end loader. (If you happen to be in the construction business and use Caterpillar products, then you may have an investing edge.)

This guideline is especially important to heed for high-tech companies. While writers for *Wired* magazine may make a killing buying high-tech companies, most of us end up as dead meat when we try that. The computer world is changing so fast, it's hard for most casual investors to keep up. If you insist on jumping into the fray, try investing in a technology mutual fund.

Stick to Quality Companies. In most industries one or a few companies develop a superior product, brand name, distribution network, and/or grow to such size and economies of scale that they dominate their market. This can happen even in reasonably low-tech endeavors such as razors or breakfast cereal. (Imagine a new razor-blade company trying to take on Gillette.) Sometimes these companies screw up and lose their edge—or the economy shifts and their business becomes obsolete—but usually their position insulates them from serious competition, further deepening their advantages. The winners keep winning, which means that about all you, as an investor, have to do is hang on for the ride. (The caveat is, if the company is a market darling, sometimes it's overvalued.)

Although it usually works out well to buy these niche-dominating companies on bad earnings news and monetary setbacks (for example, buying pharmaceutical stocks after they dropped in value on concerns over Clinton's health-care reform proposals), don't confuse that with reaching for dramatic-turnaround situations or bottom-fishing, as they say in the trade. For most investors, trying to pick survivors of business debacles is a losing strategy. It requires lots of research and monitoring, and most companies don't recover. No matter how high a company's stock price once was, a low price isn't a bargain if the business is on the road to oblivion. Be more concerned about where a company is going than where its stock price has been. If you can't resist a turn-around, at least wait until after the company has survived its worst difficulties. You won't catch it at its lowest point, but you're less likely to be caught empty-handed—or have to wait forever for its fortunes to turn.

Disregard "the Market." There is so much noise about what "the market" is doing or going to do that it's hard not to have an opinion about it or try to guess it right. There are three very good reasons to shut out all the babble: First, you should only be investing long-term money in stocks anyhow, so where your stocks are in six months shouldn't much matter. Second, you'll never have peace of mind if you try to call it just right. Third, no one can consistently predict where the market is going in the short term (over the long term, *the* prediction is up). The combination of macroeconomic forces, political events, and mass psychology that moves the market is too complex and random for anyone to forecast reliably.

Even when the market gets "expensive," it can continue to go up or just stall rather than tank. And even in expensive markets, there are usually undervalued, good companies to be found. Every outstanding investor advises ignoring all the predictions about the overall market and concentrating on whether the business you're buying represents a good value. General market sell-offs can be a good opportunity to buy great companies inexpensively. One seldom, if ever, buys stocks right at the bottom or sells right at the top.

Invest in Companies You Feel Good About. Owning stock in companies you feel good about is not only good for your conscience, it pays in the long run. One of the hardest parts of getting superior returns is having the patience to let a business's growth unfold. Sticking with a company through temporary setbacks and market sell-offs is easier if you feel comfortable owning its stock. Warren Buffett has advised that if you aren't willing to own a stock for ten years, you shouldn't own it for ten minutes.

Avoid Volatile Stocks. Volatile stocks, like volatile people, can fray your nerves. Sure, they can be exciting and rewarding at times, but in the long run, is it worth it? If you're trying to simplify your financial life, the answer is no.

Price volatility of stocks is measured by something called beta. Calculated from past price patterns, beta indicates how much a stock is expected to move in relation to the whole market. The S&P 500 index is assigned a beta of 1.00. So stocks with a beta of 1.50 are expected to move half again as much as most stocks. A .50 beta indicates a stock price that is likely to move only half as much as the general market. So a .50 beta stock would be expected to drop only 4 percent when the market dropped 8 percent (and have a similar ratio when prices increase, too). A stock with a negative beta tends to move in a direction opposite to the market. For a calmer portfolio, stick to those companies with betas under 1.00.

Several stock-tracking services, such as *Value Line* (which is available at most libraries), indicate a stock's beta.

Don't Swing at Every Pitch. If finding companies that fit the parameters of the preceding guidelines *and* have good financial prospects sounds tough, think of that as a positive.

Owning a few of the right companies is much more relaxing, generates less paperwork, and is more likely to bring better returns than having a large portfolio. If a stock doesn't fit with your scenario, don't bite—no matter how pumped your brother-in-law is about it.

By choosing carefully, you'll naturally become a buy-and-hold investor. This lowers your transaction costs and ultimately takes less time because you did it right the first time.

Discount stock commissions and Internet access to financial information have created a growing population of trading junkies. This frenetic trading is good for ulcers and carpal tunnel syndrome but not much else. The $20 you're charged to buy and sell a stock may sound like diddly, but when you round-trip a few times a day, you're $120 in the hole if your picks tread water—and that doesn't count the small loss you take buying at the ask price and selling at the bid (the difference in price between what the highest buyer and lowest seller are asking).

One of the great things about equities is, they are totally liquid, making it easy to get your money when you need it. The problem is, the constant updating of prices makes investors jumpy and hungry for action. If you were to invest in a building, you wouldn't check its value every five minutes or even every five months. Most investors would be better off only checking their stock prices when their statement came in.

THE REAL SCOOP ON SOCIALLY RESPONSIBLE INVESTING IN STOCKS

Everyone knows there are three topics to avoid if you want to keep conversation polite: politics, money, and religion. No wonder socially responsible investing, which involves elements of all three, has been a lightning rod for clashing, passionate opinions.

Ethical investing in stocks, in particular, has attracted the most controversy. This isn't surprising given that stocks and the market are the "big leagues" of finance—the blood sport, which attracts the most fans, talent, and pundit commentary. But adding confusion to the excitement is the somewhat complex, counterintuitive, and indirect nature of shareholder corporate ownership. It seems that part of the shouting is much ado about little.

A VERY SHORT HISTORY

Socially responsible investing first registered on the hip zeitgeist in the early eighties, but it's been around for a long time. Ethical investing traces its roots to seventeenth-century Quakers, who refused to invest in armament businesses, and to a decidedly unhip group, early twentieth-century teetotalers. The movement's first formal expression came from religious groups that shunned tobacco and alcohol companies.

During the Vietnam War era, socially concerned investors turned their backs on defense contractors and made the first attempts at corporate divestiture in South Africa. Shareholder activism—that is, trying to change corporate behavior through formal shareholder resolutions—developed into a potent tool.

Since then most social investors have had what the Right calls a liberal agenda, focusing on improving companies' environmental records, equal employment opportunity, and animal rights. What was once a handful of socially screened mutual funds has grown to more than fifty, including some that focus on just one major issue, such as women's and gay rights. The newest segment of the SRI genre comes from the religious fundamentalists, who have developed their own screens against corporations deemed to be "antifamily."

According to the Social Investment Forum—a Washington, D.C., trade group for socially concerned investing professionals—roughly $1 trillion, or one in every ten investing dollars, is invested with some social criteria. A dozen years ago, that total was only $40 billion, making socially responsible investing one of the fastest-growing segments of the financial services industry.

THE THREE FORMS OF SRI IN STOCKS

Most socially concerned stock investors express themselves through avoidance or negative screening. The basic principle is to invest your principal with your principles. That is, just say no to companies you disapprove of. Against animal testing? Then why be part owner of Procter & Gamble?

For many SRI investors, avoiding the bad guys isn't enough. They want to back companies that make the world a better place. You could, for example, buy shares in a toxic-cleanup firm or a company that makes vegetarian burgers. While no company is lily-white (even SRI favorites like Ben & Jerry's and The Body Shop have their critics), there is a growing cadre of businesses that do good in addition to making tidy profits.

The last—and most powerful—mode of SRI is shareholder activism: exercising your rights as a shareholder to influence corporate management.

SHAREHOLDER ACTIVISM:
FLEXING YOUR OWNERSHIP RIGHTS

Shareholder activism is the muscle in socially responsible investing. Like the fabled two-by-four whacked against a stubborn Ozark mule, it gets a corporation's attention, reaching CEOs and management otherwise inaccessible to social activists. Shareholder activism is the lever behind SRI's greatest successes, such as enlisting companies to adopt the *Valdez* principles or divesting much of corporate America from pre-Mandela South Africa.

Despite this power, shareholder activism receives much less attention than stock screening—no doubt because, like most activism, it's not a profit generator. Most SRI brokers, mutual funds, and money managers focus on picking winning, screened stocks and attracting new investors. Since shareholder activism doesn't directly produce revenues, most SRI firms don't spend resources and energy on it.

Shareholder activism is also counterintuitive—and thus not easy to market. Consider: You're upset with General Electric, one of the nation's top polluters. You won't buy a GE fridge, you refuse to watch the latest NBC (a GE subsidiary) special, and you tell everyone to boycott the corporate giant. Buying GE stock is the last thing you'd think of doing. But that's exactly what's required to take shareholder action.

As stockholder/part owner of a public corporation, you have a few rights. Even if you hold only thirty shares of GE (an ownership stake that, if GE were actually divvied up, wouldn't buy you the CEO's water closet), you still have a voice. Come annual meeting time, you can have your remedies for GE broadcast to all its shareholders. There are some formal procedures to follow first, but it's surprisingly easy to do.

To bring a proposed change in policy before GE shareholders, the Securities and Exchange Commission (SEC) requires that you own $1,000 worth of stock for at least one year prior to the resolution filing date—which is listed in the company's annual proxy statement. (That waiting period is waived if you own 1 percent of the shares outstanding.) Your resolution must be shorter than five hundred words and conform to SEC style rules. Then your statement is sent to the CEO or corporate secretary with proof of ownership, and voilà! Your suggestion will be on the next annual shareholder agenda.

Of course, the hard part is garnering enough votes to actually change policies. Start by working with the Interfaith Center on Corporate Responsibility (ICCR: [212] 870-2295) and Investor Responsibility Research Center (IRRC: [202] 833-0700). ICCR and IRRC coordinate the efforts of progressive shareholder activists. They can help phrase your resolution and then spread the word by publishing it in their journal, which goes to like-minded investors.

If you publicize your resolution well and get at least 3 percent of the shareholder vote, you can resubmit it the following year. In subsequent years you need 6 percent of the vote and then at least 10 percent thereafter to keep it on the ballot. Failing to get those minimums means you must wait three years to bring up that resolution again.

Tim Smith, director of ICCR for over thirty years, points out, "Even if a resolution doesn't pass—as most don't—it can still have considerable influence. In fact, it is very likely that the greater impact is not from resolutions voted on, but from resolutions withdrawn as a result of successful negotiations."

Management wants smooth annual meetings and fears the negative publicity that comes from an embarrassing public agenda. Often, a corporation will be willing to consult with activists to avoid having the resolution appear at all.

Even if you don't file a resolution yourself, pay attention to those on annual proxy statements. In addition to casting a ballot for those with an enlightened bent, write a letter to the CEO; express your concern and explain why you voted as you did. If you can make it to the annual meeting, raise issues directly to management during shareholder question time. Have a good grasp of the issue first, but don't assume someone else will speak up if you don't. It's partly your company. Have your say.

WHAT ABOUT RETURNS?
DO SRI INVESTORS HAVE TO SUFFER?

The mainstream financial media have largely evaluated ethical investing based on returns. Throughout the mid-nineties, when most SRI *growth* funds lagged behind the market averages, the social screeners took a beating in the financial press. *The Wall Street Journal, Money,* and *Forbes,* to name just a few, ran columns carrying headlines such as GOOD INTENTIONS, BAD RESULTS and IT'S NOT EASY BEING GREEN. These articles typically portrayed socially concerned investors as good-hearted saps condemned to everlasting lousy returns.

What these authors seem to forget is that, just a few years before, the same publications were sprinkled with headlines such as DOING WELL BY DOING GOOD. SRI wasn't endorsed with quite the gusto it later got panned with, but it was often suggested that superior investing returns resulted from ethical screens. This idea was originally popularized by *Good*

Money publisher Dr. Ritchie Lowry. Lowry figured that social screening improved investing performance because ethical companies are less likely to be sued and tend to be fiscally conservative.

Serious research hasn't supported either claim. The truth is, social screens have little or no impact on investing results. As Santa Clara University professor of finance Meir Statman concluded, "Social screening affects performance as much as screening out companies with left-handed CEOs."

THE REAL PROBLEM

Ironically, what few SRI critics point out is that *as it is usually practiced*, investing in stocks with social screens has a negligible effect on making the world a better place. The SRI industry battle cry, "Vote with your investing dollars," is misleading.

The trouble is, social issues are not on the referendum. When you buy stock in a public company, it doesn't go directly to the company itself but to another investor (or other investors). Your investment only reaches a public company when it first goes public or issues new equity—increasingly a rarity, as more public corporations are now buying back their own shares rather than issuing them.

What the stock market really votes on is a company's monetary value. A corporation's stock price reflects its ability (or perceived future ability) to produce profits. A stock boycott of a company will only briefly affect its stock price as long as its business remains strong.

When a company's stock price is relatively low for its profits, it makes an appealing investment for anyone looking to maximize returns and minimize risk. Every SRI money manager seeks to do exactly that; he or she just avoids doing it with unsavory companies. Ultimately, it's the desire for the best returns that makes social questions (except when expressed fiscally as the fear of lawsuits—as has been the case for cigarette makers) unregisterable in the stock market.

Even if every investor were socially concerned, a nice company with an idealistic mission will still see its stock plunge if it consistently reports losses. A solar-panel manufacturer earning $50,000 a year is worth more than one earning $5,000 a year, whether you're an environmentalist or Rush Limbaugh.

Perversely, screening out unenlightened companies without taking legislative, legal, or public relations action actually monetarily rewards investors who buy the "outcasts." Consider a thriving porn shop: if no one wants to buy it, its price will drop until it's available for a song. The eventual new owner would then receive an unusually high return on his investment.

"That's fine and good for some creep," you may be thinking, "but I have no interest in making money from a porn shop—or cigarette company, for that matter." Therein lies the crux of the case for social screening: it's a moral expression—but that by itself will not produce any change in the world.

Not investing in a porn palace doesn't affect its operation or turn the tide against objectifying women. To do that, don't patronize the shop; convince others to boycott it, too; or shut it down through legal channels.

THE BOTTOM LINE: WHAT SRI IN STOCKS CAN DO

Deflating the claims of social-screening promoters doesn't mean social screening is a sham; it's simply been given more buildup than warranted. Screening doesn't produce change the way advocacy does, but it still has its place—as long as investors understand its true purpose and don't fool themselves into thinking screening alone makes a difference.

Screening is psychologically valuable. If you own stock in a company that builds nuclear power plants, it's harder to oppose nuke construction. And more to the point, while refusing to profit from exploitive companies doesn't change them (unless you're doing shareholder activism), it lets you sleep at night. It maintains the consistency, and thus the dignity, of your principles—which obviously no one can put a price tag on.

To go beyond being able to sleep, you need to make your voice heard. Shareholder activism has proved a good way to do that, regardless of the size of your holdings. Large shareholders, such as mutual funds and pension funds, don't even have to wait until annual meetings to be heard by management. Sign on with money managers who are willing to make waves, and encourage others to do the same.

If you had to make a choice between a fund that screens or does advocacy work (and many funds emphasize one or the other), which should you go for? Personally, I'd choose advocacy. Even if you own a "feel-bad" company like Anheuser-Busch, you can still make some positive changes. No, you won't talk it out of the liquor business, but you could conceivably get it to lay off marketing to teens, improve its environmental record, increase funding for treating alcoholism, and become a more enlightened employer. That wouldn't eliminate drunk driving, but it would make the world a slightly better place.

Of course, only you know whether you'll really exercise your shareholder voice; only you can judge the psychological value of avoiding offensive companies; only you can draw the line on what you consider a destructive company. No company is perfect, as some SRI debunkers like to point out: all pollute at least somewhat; almost all are run by white males. Rather than mess with those questions, some ask, why not just get the best returns you can and give away profits to good causes? I've certainly heard lots worse ideas—if you really do it. Being a pragmatist, I'd even favor it over screening alone.

Sure, playing the stock game with a social conscience makes it more complicated, but you'll make your decisions at least with your eyes open.

REAL ESTATE

Real estate development swings both ways: it can be destructive or progressive. The bad guys put up a golf course and condos that trash wetlands and leak sewage into the water supply. The good guys do an environmentally sensitive rehab, revitalizing a flagging urban area. Most projects lie somewhere in between, of course, but should offer the opportunity to at least make small, yet significant improvements, such as investing in energy efficiency or being a humane landlord.

There are two basic ways to invest in real estate: buy it and manage it yourself or let others do it for you. Although having professionals handle it doesn't guarantee a profit, it will at least be hassle-free.

THE REIT STUFF

The easiest way to get professional management is through a real estate investment trust (REIT)—the stock market's answer to investing in real estate. REITs are publicly traded stocks that invest in office buildings, apartment complexes, nursing homes, and other commercial spaces. As with a stock mutual fund, investors pool their money and hope to benefit from the expertise of a professional real estate money manager—who can buy properties and diversify in a way the small investor never could. Management fees are relatively low since real estate trusts invest such large sums. Perhaps best of all, unlike property you purchase yourself, a REIT is totally liquid and can be sold at any time. It can also be added to in increments as small as the REIT's share price.

To maintain their special tax benefits, REITs must pass on 95 percent of each year's operating profits in regular dividend payments. The typical REIT offers a much higher yield than the average stock. The high yield doesn't preclude appreciation, though, as long as the properties in a trust's portfolio increase in value. An index of REIT stocks actually outperformed the S&P 500 over the last ten years.

Naturally, a REIT stock can head south just as an equity can—a likely scenario if the properties depreciate, rental income dries up, or stocks in general sell off. REITs tend to fluctuate in price along with the whole market. As a result, REITs don't work as an inflation hedge the way owning real estate outright does.

REITs invest in a wide variety of real estate projects, so avoid those putting up strip malls in favor of progressive projects. This is particularly important when investing in a new offering, as your investment will directly fund something you'd be proud or ashamed of. Contact a socially responsible investing broker and ask to be alerted when new, kosher REITs come out. Be sure to read the prospectus first. Not surprisingly, the number of REITs putting up affordable housing for the elderly is far outnumbered by conventional developers.

Many money guides suggest investing in REIT mutual funds, but this doesn't make sense—even if you don't care about the type of properties the REIT invests in (there are no SRI REITs). A mutual fund provides professional management and diversification; that's exactly what an individual REIT is already set up for. Why pay an extra management fee?

THE LIMITS OF LIMITED PARTNERSHIPS

As with a REIT, investors in a limited partnership combine their money for increased buying power and savvy management—in this case, the pro is called the general partner. Unlike a REIT, limited partnerships offer tax benefits in addition to a chance for appreciation. The tax savings come from depreciation and the lower tax rates levied on long-term gains (for details on how it works, see pages 77–78).

Limited partnerships, however, have problems REITs don't—namely, *serious* sales and management fees and a lack of liquidity. Limited partnership fees purchased through your friendly broker can gobble up 20-plus percent of your investment before it's converted to bricks and mortar. And should you need the money before the partnership expires (a typical life is ten years), "Fuhget about it." Occasionally there's an unofficial secondary market, but even then you'd be offered a ridiculously low price. The notable exception to this is for tax-credit housing partnerships, which are popular for corporations seeking tax credits and for ethical investors.

Tax-credit housing partnerships come in two main varieties: low-income housing and historic rehabilitation. Although the details differ in each, the lowdown is that the government, in an effort to draw money to these worthwhile projects, offers tax *credits* on your investment. (Note: A tax credit is much better than a deduction. Every dollar of credit directly reduces the taxes you owe—a $1,500 credit, for example, lops $1,500 from your tax bill.) For those in the upper income tax brackets (but not too high, as couples making over $250,000 and singles over $200,000 can't participate), the tax benefits can offer high rates of return.

DOING IT YOURSELF

Buying and managing property yourself gives more control, better tax benefits, and a better shot at big profits than turning the job over to someone else; the downside is, it takes lots more work. Rental property—which is the only real estate your average part-timer should invest in—entails, well, dealing with renters. This might mean just one renter if you let a house or dozens if you own a small apartment complex. Naturally, when the boiler breaks, the roof leaks, the neighbors fight, or a rent check bounces, you're the one in the middle.

Historically, investing in real estate has offered investment returns that are competitive with stocks—and, happily, with less volatility. Real estate investing is also easier to understand than the stock market. Most of us have an intuitive sense for our local real estate market and thus a property's value. Judging whether a smallish rental unit is a good buy is a lot easier than assessing a company whose industry and intricate accounting you can hardly follow.

To check out a building, talk to the current tenants, the neighbors, the town clerk, and the police department. Walk the streets and poke around in the basement. All these give clues to whether you're inheriting ye ol' lemon or scooping up a peach. The decentralized market for properties gives you a chance of picking up a bargain, sold by an uninformed or cash-hungry owner.

When you own your own place, you have direct control over how the building is run. You don't need to appeal to the CEO or board of directors to treat tenants well or make sure the property is environmentally friendly. Owning real estate gives the opportunity to beautify your small corner of the world.

Clearly, the preceding advice is only designed to give you a taste of whether buying a rental property appeals to you. Before making a down payment, do research and read a few books on the topic. Borrowing money to buy a property can make a small investment really pay off. Or it can mean you end up with losses even greater than your down payment. Leverage cuts both ways, so make sure you know what you're doing.

SAVINGS GOALS

RETIREMENT

Most articles about retirement planning fall into two camps: those that make you feel bad and those that make you feel really bad. The really bad ones start by having us imagine a J. Crewesque retirement—sailing from a Martha's Vineyard beach house in the summer, wine tasting in France in the spring, and shuttling between Jackson Hole and an uncrowded Caribbean island in the winter. Then we're shown a chart with lots of figures. These numbers inevitably lead to a nose-bleeding total indicating just how much money we'll need to underwrite a "comfortable" retirement. And by the way, we're told, forget about help from Social Security; better just turn your paycheck over to your nearest five-star mutual fund.

The conclusion we draw is, hello, o.t. and Amway moonlighting; good-bye, joie de vivre. Ditto after reading the run-of-the-mill, disheartening retirement piece—the only difference is the grand total is slightly lower and the exotic backdrops are missing.

These articles turn us prematurely gray for two reasons: First, they tap into our fears about old age. Rather than face those directly, we slip into the classic American response to any problem: buy a solution—as if throwing money at old age would take care of everything. Second, we haven't stopped and reflected on our later years realistically—in terms of both the vitality we can expect to have and how much money we'll need. You need to figure your retirement scenario based on your own estimates. Remember, those frightening projections in *Worth* magazine assume you're maintaining a $90,000-a-year set-up.

A holistic approach to retirement focuses first on quality of life and nonfinancial investments in our health, passions, and relationships. These efforts may not show up on your Citibank account, but—in addition to their obvious intrinsic value—they pay real financial dividends. Good health reduces medical bills and extends our working life and our ability to care for ourselves; active interests keep us vital and allow us to earn money from work we care about; and a strong network of family and friends means we can receive care and assistance without having to hire out. (The Amish have such a strong community-support system for their elderly that they refuse help from Medicare and Medicaid.)

Much of our thinking about retirement and aging is simply outdated. The classic retirement age of sixty-five has no correlation to our biological clock but is a relic from the nineteenth century and Otto von Bismarck. The German prime minister wanted to offer his civil servants pensions—as long as it didn't cost the government much. He originally proposed paying benefits at age seventy but compromised on sixty-five. Either way, Bismarck had a good deal since life expectancy back then was less than forty-five. Now we're living longer than ever and are healthier than ever but are still stuck with the sixty-five mentality.

While the body's aging process is no picnic, we imagine

we'll be worse off in our old age than the facts bear out. Even the elderly have a warped perception: a Lou Harris survey of senior citizens found that 40 percent believed that illness afflicted old people in general, even though only 21 percent said they'd been sick themselves. According to the National Academy of Science, the actual number of those over sixty-five in poor health is only 15 percent. Forty-five percent of the polled elders also felt certain that most of their peers suffered loneliness, but only 13 percent reported being lonely themselves.

The truth of our increased longevity still hasn't shown up in the way we see ourselves. We need to readjust our thinking about retirement—and thus how we live our whole life. Right now many of us are in a kind of panicked race against the clock, working late, cutting short time with our kids, and fretting that we won't have money enough come age sixty-five. But we have more time than we think; most of us will be able to keep working well past sixty-five. One reason Americans are eager to retire young is that they're burned out. If we slowed down now and stuck to work we found meaningful, we'd want to keep working—and thus earning—well after our odometer hit old-timer territory. Surveys show that retirees consistently wish that they had more fulfilling work and less free time on their hands.

A recent study on exercise and aging indicates that those who live sedentary lives need assisted living ten to twenty years sooner than those who exercise. When you consider that nursing homes cost between $40,000 and $70,000 a year, even if you use low-end estimates (and don't factor in inflation), keeping fit can save $400,000 (in after-tax dollars).

Staying healthy and active is like having money in the

bank. After retiring, you have more time to do what you once paid others for. When you're healthy, you can cut the lawn yourself, fix the porch steps, bake bread, or grow tomatoes. It may not be glamorous, but saving on "the little things" adds up, and more important, taking care of yourself keeps you engaged in life (even more so than jetting to vacation spots).

Framed in financial terms, your vitality is an excellent hedge against inflation. And inflation—as every financial consultant knows—is a serious consideration when planning for retirement, since it eats away at the buying power of savings. But what few financial advisers tell us is that inflation doesn't affect all costs equally. A closer look shows that much of inflation's "damage" comes from increases in health-care and labor costs. (Many products, such as computers, bicycles, or stereos, actually drop in price over time—especially when you hang back from the cutting edge: first-generation computers with Pentium processors, for example, cost a fraction of what they did a few years ago, and a 286 or 386 machine that's great for word-processing sells for maybe $100.) Good health helps you sidestep or mitigate both the health-care and labor-cost aspects of inflation.

Of course, there are no guarantees when it comes to our well-being. You could eat macrobiotic your whole life and still get Alzheimer's. Or you could make a dedicated commitment to your marriage and children and still end up divorced or estranged. But there's also no guarantee that your savings won't be thrashed by a currency devaluation, hyperinflation, or a stock market crash.

So before taking on extra work and stress to pay for your retirement, think long and hard. Cutting expenses is usually the better way to go. The *real* bottom line is, if you get Alzheimer's, a fat portfolio won't mean anything to you anyhow. Being healthy at eighty is worth a whole lot more than being rich at eighty.

FIGURING HOW MUCH YOU NEED

Of course, even the most robust of souls should plan financially for retirement. You may not need annual cruises, but you will need some income—no matter how much you like do-it-yourself projects. The questions are, how much, and where will it come from? Answering these questions can dissipate fears about how you're going to manage.

For those who hate filling out even simple worksheets, an easy retirement savings rule of thumb is to put away 10 percent of your gross income each year starting when you are in your twenties and thirties. The snafu, of course, is that life often intervenes. In your twenties you may be paying off student loans or not making enough to stash away 10 percent. In your thirties you're likely to be incurring the extra expenses that go with parenthood. If you've been thrown off "schedule," or have an unorthodox financial life, doing the calculation presented in this subsection is the best way to get a good guesstimate as to how much you need to save.

The first step is to do a budget of what you would expect to spend if you were retired today. Keep in mind that your expenses are likely to drop considerably. If you own a home, your mortgage will probably be paid off. If you have kids, they're apt to be on their own. You won't have work clothes and commuting to pay for. And entertainment costs should go down (on average by 50 percent); after all, you won't need peak-season, expensive vacations. In many ways your cost-of-living situation is most analogous to a debt-free college graduate, whose life, if you recall, can be managed on a shoestring.

Funding your retirement budget will come from some combination of savings, work, Social Security, a pension, and/or an inheritance. Although Social Security does have problems and should be reformed, the predictions of its bankruptcy are overblown. When spending on Medicare—where projections of fiscal viability do look truly alarming—is separated from the cost of Social Security benefits, the figures don't look so bad. Even if no reforms were introduced between now and 2029, the government would still be able to send out checks worth three-quarters of today's benefits to all retirees for the next fifty years. And given the number of aging boomers, it's hard to imagine there won't be reforms. After all, if you think the American Association of Retired Persons (AARP) lobby is strong now, picture it on steroids in a few years.

So while you shouldn't rely on a full Social Security income, it is likely you'll get something.[1] Keep in mind, though, that even at its best, Social Security was only intended as a subsistence income. Unless you're a master of self-sufficiency or frugality, you'll want income beyond what the feds provide.

The following chart gives you a rough idea of what you can expect in Social Security benefits in today's dollars. For a more accurate figure, contact the Social Security Administration directly, at (800) 772-1213, and ask for Form 7004. It

---

1. Most likely those with substantial savings will get less Social Security than they do now or owe some taxes on the money they do get, and the official retirement/benefits age will climb—as it already has if you were born after 1960.

only takes a couple of minutes to fill out. A few weeks later, you'll receive a record of your reported earnings and an estimate of what your benefits will be.

YOUR EXPECTED SOCIAL SECURITY BENEFITS (IN 1997 DOLLARS)

AVERAGE ANNUAL EARNINGS	APPROXIMATE MONTHLY BENEFIT
$10,000	$540
$20,000	$775
$30,000	$1,020
$40,000	$1,100
$58,000+	$1,200

Note that these payouts are for individual earners. If your spouse didn't work, he or she will receive 50 percent of what you collect.

RETIREMENT-PLANNING WORKSHEET

Since a lot can change between now and your retirement—namely, inflation and your earnings—financial projections for your sunset years are at best approximations. Because of these variables, the calculations can be an involved and tricky business or relatively simple. I've tried to keep the number crunching as easy as possible, figuring (1) then you'll be more likely to do it and (2) no matter how sophisticated a spreadsheet you use to calculate variables, you eventually must settle on one best-guess scenario anyhow. The big assumption for the following worksheet is that your investments will grow 4 percent faster per year than inflation. Historically that has been quite achievable, but clearly that could change.

HOW MUCH TO SAVE FOR RETIREMENT

1. Amount of yearly income in today's dollars you'd need to retire now. (Note: See explanation earlier in this subsection as to why this is likely to be less than you need now.)

$_____ per year

2. Expected annual Social Security benefits. (If you want to be conservative and were born after 1960, reduce official estimates by 75 percent.)

− $_____ per year

3. Yearly pension benefits, if any. (If your benefits won't increase with inflation during retirement, multiply by 60 percent.)

− $_____ per year

4. Amount, if any, you guess you'd earn from hobbies or part-time work after "retiring."

− $_____ per year

5. Yearly income you'll need from personal savings (line 1 minus lines 2, 3, and 4).

= $_____ per year

6. To get the savings total   ×   19
you'll need to retire at age   = $_____ total
66, multiply line 5 by 19.   savings needed

7. Your current net worth. $_____

8. To discover what your sav-   ×   _____ growth
ings will be worth by retire-   multiplier
ment time, multiply line 7   = $_____
by the *growth multiplier* from
the accompanying table.

9. Amount you still need to
save (line 6 minus line 8).   = $_____

10. How much you need to
save each month (multiply $_____ amount to
line 9 by the appropriate   save per month
savings factor from the third
column of the accompanying
table).

YOUR CURRENT AGE	GROWTH MULTIPLIER	SAVINGS FACTOR FACTOR
26	4.8	.001
28	4.4	.001
30	4.1	.001
32	3.8	.001
34	3.5	.001
36	3.2	.001
38	3.0	.002
40	2.8	.002
42	2.6	.002
44	2.4	.002
46	2.2	.003
48	2.0	.003
50	1.9	.004
52	1.7	.005
54	1.6	.006
56	1.5	.007
58	1.4	.009
60	1.3	.013
62	1.2	.020
64	1.1	.041

Reprinted with permission from Eric Tyson's *Personal Finance for Dummies.*

THE COLLEGE-FUNDING CHALLENGE

For many parents the price of college looms like a Himalayan mountain. And with good reason. In 1998 elite private schools cost more than $30,000 a year. Looking forward, things only get worse: college fees are likely to increase faster than inflation—as they have for the last twenty years (though at a less torrid pace).

For children born in 1996, a four-year Ivy League degree will cost an estimated $300,000—literally a Mount Everest–sized string of twenty-dollar notes attached end-to-end. By then, even public college degrees are projected to cost $100,000—a figure that is attainable with one child if you're disciplined, focused, and plan a route well. But with two or more children to fund, not to mention retirement, what's a body to do?

Before getting vertigo, note a few things: First, remember why you want your child to have a liberal arts education in the first place. Qualities such as intellectual curiosity, an ability to learn on his or her own, and a basic breadth of knowledge can be picked up outside a university. Trading essential quality time with your kids for overtime to pay for college doesn't make sense, especially when they are young and really need you. The most important thing we can give our children is emotional nourishment; advanced degrees are gravy—not part of the core curriculum.

Second, your own retirement savings come first—at least certain minimums that ensure you're on track (see the retirement-planning worksheet on page 127). This may sound selfish, but it will stretch your savings. Financial aid officers don't expect you to contribute IRS-approved retirement savings to fund college. So adding to an IRA instead of a college fund actually increases the chances that your child will get aid or a scholarship.

Third, most financial fancy footwork and investment products marketed to college savers are marginally helpful, if at all; ignore them. Either they're a rip-off, such as expensive scholarship search services (you can get the same thing for free on the Internet), or they work best for those who can already afford tuition. Putting savings in your kid's name, for example, makes sense for those in the highest tax brackets who won't qualify for financial aid, but it is a bad idea for anyone who plans to apply.

Fourth, you don't need to come up with every penny. Most college financial experts applaud anyone who's put away half the cash necessary to pay for college. Financial aid packages and loans can usually carry you the rest of the way.

And finally, some schools cost lots less than others; be willing to explore alternatives.

THE BASIC INVESTING STRATEGY

For any long-term savings goal, you'll get the same basic advice over and over: the earlier you start, the better. Put the cosmic law of compounding interest to work for you and start saving as soon as possible. Most new parents react to that advice with: "Get real, dude; saving when you have a baby or toddler? Didn't you ever hear about child-care costs and career sabbaticals?" Of course, I have; I know that coming up with extra dough in the early years is especially tough. If you're not able to put anything away until your child is, say, age ten, then pick up the advice in this subsection for starting at that age.

If you happen to have something set aside to invest for college or if grandparents have made a contribution, head to the stock market. The simplest method is to stick with the Domini Social Index fund. With so many years until tuition bills, time is on your side, and you needn't worry about short-term setbacks in the stock market.

Around age ten until fourteen, new savings should be invested more conservatively. A mutual fund, like Pax World, that invests in stocks and bonds or high-yielding stocks is an easy, one-stop option. Since tuition payments aren't that far away, you want lower volatility without relinquishing the chance for the higher returns stocks offer.

When your scholar-to-be hits fourteen, it's time to be more cautious, as you may never recover from stock market hiccups. Try for a fifty-fifty split between stocks and CDs (or tax-free bonds if you're in a high tax bracket) that mature when tuition is due. Those in the 28 to 31 percent bracket can benefit from buying U.S. government EE bonds, as their interest is tax-free when used to pay for college. (If you're in the 15 percent bracket, the tax savings aren't worth more than the lower interest these bonds pay.) Since EE bonds pay higher rates when you hold them at least five years, purchase them with money earmarked for the sophomore year.

By the time your child is seventeen, only a quarter of the money should be in the stock market.

One caveat: Be careful about the timing of liquidating profits from your college funds or any other investments. Capital gains that show up on your income tax during your child's junior year of high school (assuming your child applies for financial aid during the fall of her senior year) will be treated by financial aid officers as income. If the gain is substantial, it could reduce the financial aid you're eligible for.

FIGURING HOW MUCH YOU NEED TO SAVE

The worksheet in this subsection shows how much you'll need to put away, depending upon when you start saving.

As already noted, if you can put away 50 percent of the total while also funding your retirement, you're doing all right—certainly way better than most. Between student loans, grants, financial aid, and your own borrowing, you'll finesse it.

To figure out what you should save every month, you need to know the cost of the college your child will attend. In 1998 the approximate four-year cost for an expensive, Ivy League–type degree was $135,000; for the average private college, $95,000; and for the average state school, $46,000. These totals include tuition, fees, room, board, and other expenses.

By knowing today's college costs, you can easily figure your necessary savings, since after-tax investment returns and college inflation are growing at roughly the same rate. Obviously, if one or the other doesn't keep pace, you'll have either a shortfall or a windfall. To be perfectly accurate, you should redo this worksheet once a year, accounting for the increase in college costs. The rule of thumb is to increase the cost of college by 5 or 6 percent a year.

HOW MUCH TO SAVE FOR COLLEGE

1. Today's cost of the college that you think your child will attend.

$\$$_____

2. Percentage of college you'd like to pay for.

$\times$ _____%

3. Amount you'd pay in today's dollars.

= $\$$_____

4. Number of months until your child goes to college (years left $\times$ 12 + any extra months left).

_____ months

5. Amount you need to save per month (divide line 3 by line 4).

$\$$_____ per month

ALTERNATIVE ROUTES

Getting a Job with Your Child's College. Most colleges offer free or reduced tuition for the children of employees. This includes all jobs—from lawn maintenance to administrators. Some colleges even have reciprocal arrangements with other schools. When you consider how much you'd have to earn after taxes to put aside the $10,000 to $30,000 a year (in 1998 dollars) this nets you, you could take a large pay cut and still do well financially by working at the right school. Clearly, there are other considerations involved in whether this is a wise move, but it's an option to consider.

Your Child's Working. Gone are the days when part-time minimum-wage jobs and hustling in the summer could underwrite a bachelor's degree. But when a teenager contributes to his own college costs, it does wonders for his commitment and appreciation for the degree.

A *Money* magazine national survey of one thousand undergraduates found "that working up to 10 hours a week did not diminish either satisfaction or academic achievement. Above 10 hours, however, both dropped markedly." So if your kid needs to log in lots of working hours, have her do it in the summer or by taking a year or two off before attending school full-time. Do note, however, that some campus jobs, such as dormitory resident adviser, not only pay a small stipend, they provide free room and board—in effect creating well-paying jobs when the after-tax cost is considered.

If your student has a clear idea of her eventual vocation, she can actually be paid for work and earn credits at the same time. There are almost a thousand two- and four-year colleges that offer a co-op education program. Students earn as much as $8,000 a year plus college credits working part-time in their anticipated field.

School Choice. Perhaps the biggest effect your child can have on the cost of his education is in his school selection. Naturally, there can be considerable differences between schools, particularly in specialized fields. But the disparity in a liberal arts education offered at most respected universities and the top Ivy League schools isn't nearly as much as the prestige would imply. To quote my brother, who attended three different colleges and graduated with an Ivy League diploma, "No matter where you go, for every four classes you take, you get one outstanding prof, two mediocre, and one who should have stuck to research."

Starting at a community college (not necessarily in your hometown) and then transferring to a four-year school is the cheapest—if not necessarily most appealing—option. Next come state schools within your state. If staying close to home is unappealing, consider establishing residency in the state of a public university that you'd want to attend. This move has the dual benefit of lowering tuition and making it easier to get in. The University of California at Berkeley, for example, is about as hard to get into as Harvard for out-of-staters. For Californians it's no cakewalk, but attainable for good students.

Establishing residency in a new state typically means living there for a year before applying to school; it's also a good opportunity for your child to earn extra funds for college and deepen her appreciation of a university education-to-be.

Less Expensive Credits. If Gertrude Stein were an admissions officer, she'd say, "A credit is a credit is a credit." But the cost of those credits can vary widely. Even at the same college, two freshmen entering at the same time can have significantly different costs for their degree.

Those cheaper credits can be earned by taking advanced-placement courses in high school; getting transferable credits from other, less expensive institutions; taking a heavier course load so the student graduates early; or taking classes at off-hours or off-season (summer courses and weekend or night courses often cost less). Nearly two hundred colleges now have official three-year liberal arts degrees. Typically, these programs cost 17 percent less than the four-year program.

Last, less costly degrees are available by correspondence. While some correspondence schools are degree mills, many well-known institutions, such as the University of Maryland, offer legitimate credits through their program. As the Internet expands, no doubt more study and options will be possible through it.

PART 3

SPENDING IT

THE BALANCING ACT

You can tell a fair bit about a person by how he spends his money. Walk through someone's house with the eyes of a detective and you'll find ample evidence of the person's priorities, attitudes, and indulgences. Did money go into books, degrees, and art or a satellite dish and Rolex watch? What type of food is in the fridge? The point isn't to judge but to look at our own habits with a beginner's mind. Watch for patterns in your house that may be wearing you down. See if you're spending in ways that don't reflect what you really care about.

Most of us focus on the inflow of our money. We chase after raises, bonuses, and increasing sales—imagining that if only we had more, we'd have enough. Of course, it usually doesn't work that way. At some point, we need to make choices about our outflow, decisions that will take pressure off the urge for more. Part of that comes from developing some spending savvy, part of it from learning we don't need so much to be content.

Spending money well isn't like being on a restrictive diet (although many do need to cut back). A tight grip that counts pennies is no better than a regimen that requires starving. A holistic spender is in balance, not afraid to enjoy and share his wealth but also not a puppet to consumer whims. Like a healthier eater, a healthy spender follows some basic guidelines, aware of the effects of her consumption— yet also free to "indulge" occasionally. Ultimately, though, you wouldn't want to regularly spend on junk and buy things you don't need any more than you'd want to eat junk and too many calories.

Spending money thoughtfully takes integrity. It's a commitment to principles, to creating a positive ripple effect beyond your own life. You may rarely see the immediate, tangible "results" of those actions, but you'll feel them. You'll know you're in that healthy spending zone.

This section is designed to help you find that place.

THE CONSUMPTION PROBLEM

Unless Rush Limbaugh censors your media intake, you've heard that consumerism is bad for the earth. After all, name a headlined environmental problem—whether it's global warming, acid rain, ozone depletion, or habitat loss—and you'll find that the consumer lifestyle contributes a byline. Every product, no matter how neatly packaged, requires converting an animal, a vegetable, or a mineral into merchandise—an inherently energy-depleting and polluting process.

Just consider that it takes something like 76,000 trees to produce one week's edition of the Sunday *New York Times*. Add to that accounting the dioxin used for bleaching the paper, the coal burned to power the printing presses, and the gasoline burned for newsstand delivery. Without even counting the reader's drive to pick up the paper or sales from Saks ads, it becomes apparent how one "small" weekly event can have a significant effect.

Optimists tell us not to worry: energy-efficient, low-impact materials and production can fix the problem. Newspapers will be beamed to us on ultraportable computers. Clean-burning hydrogen will replace petrol, food will be grown in a

petri dish, and silicon chips made from sand will replace almost everything else.

Resource-saving technology may be our best chance for a
sustainable economy, but it's unclear whether technofixes
ever really work. "Solutions" usually leave another problem
in their wake. The Internet, for example, makes telecommut-
ing easier, reducing traffic and its associated pollution, but it
also allows more people to live in rural areas, spurring the
building of new and second homes, which gobble up forest
and farmland.

Even ignoring the law of unintended consequences, who
knows if there's enough time to incorporate beneficial tech-
nologies? Entrenched industries resist and lobby against new
alternatives, no matter how environmentally friendly. Current estimates suggest that, to create a sustainable economy
within the next forty years, we need a twentyfold improvement in the environmental performance of current technolo-
gies. With so far to go, why put all our hopes on technology?

More important, no matter how clever or resource-saving
our inventions, they can't save us from ourselves; they can't
give us meaning or create a sense of community. This is obvious enough, except we seem blind to it. No belief influences
our government's policies or our culture more than the notion that you can buy happiness. And if we're honest, it's
an idea that holds enormous sway on each of us, too. When
we pause and face that truth, most of us recognize that's no
way to live or run a country, but it's rare that we slow down;
instead, much of our lives revolves around seeking greater
comfort—which often includes getting better and more
stuff. What we miss seeing is that we've practically turned
into cartoon characters, so busy trying to get comfortable we
never rest.

Americans spend more time shopping than the Russians did during the era of infamous interminable lines in the seventies and eighties. To pay off those retail adventures we work long hours, leaving little time to enjoy our conveniences, friends, or family. And the leisure we do have is hard to enjoy; it's so valuable that we don't want to "waste" it in idleness. (Economist E. F. Schumacher posited an economic law that says: "The amount of genuine leisure available to a society is generally in inverse proportion to the amount of labor-saving machinery it employs.")

Institutions, paid help, and entertainment now often fill in for what were once family duties such as child care or tending to sick parents. On average, Americans spend nine times more time shopping than playing with their kids.

The big "winners" of our consuming economy are the largest corporations, which are raking in more at the same time they're employing less. Greater power is concentrated in fewer hands—hands that are motivated by the proverbial bottom line and, for the most part, live in isolated and privileged communities.

The have-not neighborhoods are further marginalized, receiving the polluting end of the consuming process and less support for schools, job training, and services. (The taxes spent on highways, airports, and corporate subsidies that largely benefit wealthier citizens are rarely mentioned when looking at "the cost of the poor" in an overall budget.) Our economic classes are stretched further apart. No wonder there's such resentment and violence. No wonder most of us feel economically vulnerable.

Unfortunately, the most popular way to combat those feelings of insecurity is by trying to create some *joie de Visa.*

There are other choices.

THE YIN/YANG
SPENDING SOLUTION

Our spending lives are out of balance. Typically, what's missing is restraint: we buy too much stuff, burdening the earth as well as our personal, economic lives. Call it a lack of yin, the strength from yielding or no-action.

No matter what you call it, few greet a suggestion for restraint with much enthusiasm, even if you're convinced a realignment is necessary. Restraint sounds about as much fun as dieting—and less rewarding, since thinner MasterCard bills won't elicit kudos like a flat tummy.

Deprivation diets don't work, of course—whether for eating or for spending. You may see dramatic results for a week or a few months, but in the long run, they make us feel worse and apt to binge. Like eating well or getting in shape, for healthier spending you should concentrate on the rewards of the process. After feeling more relaxed and energetic, you'll naturally want to stick with the makeover.

To sustain a consumer cutback, consciously focus on the benefits: less clutter, more free time, fewer worries, and the sense of being content with what you've got. When you reduce your spending, reward yourself with real, nonmaterial gains. Give yourself more time to do the nourishing things you've been longing for—whether that's a walk in the woods, playing with your kids, reading, or taking a meditation retreat.

And for those moments when soul-points aren't enough to keep you on the wagon, remember, you do get one tangible prize for your restraint: a larger savings account.

If saving money is your only goal, however, you'll focus too much on withholding or, to stick with the Taoist interpretation, you'll embody too much yin energy. This is almost as unhealthy as having no restraint, or too much yang. Ironically, a fixation on *not* spending can make you almost as obsessed about stuff as a crass materialist.

Consider the classic skinflint, who builds a life around saving money and stretching a budget. At the moment, the best known of this ilk is Amy Dacyczyn, aka "the *Tightwad Gazette* lady."

After the media discovered that Ms. D. could save $7,000 a year and raise a large family on a $30,000 income, she landed on more talk shows than Sly Stallone, building a successful newsletter business and selling enough books to make her a millionaire. Despite this lifetime security (or four lifetimes, given her budget), she still fills her weekends driving to tag sales, much of her weekday evenings sorting bargains she scored, and her thoughts scheming about saving money. She won't give her kids music lessons and sports activities, dismissing them as indulgences, and feeds her family out-of-date marshmallows, expired containers of ice cream, and stale corn bread from the local liquidation center.

My goal isn't to embarrass Ms. Dacyczyn, who can be quite creative in her parsimony and is probably a very nice person, but to show that she isn't the paradigm of the healthy and environmentally friendly spending that she's been promoted as—both by herself and in the alternative press.

Even *Your Money or Your Life* authors and advanced souls Joe Dominguez and Vicki Robin, who stress thriftiness as a means to achieving freedom and an uncluttered inner life, seem to miss the fact that being cheap isn't always the environmentally friendly or healthy thing to do. The dynamic duo have championed their frugal ways as good for the planet, yet they recommend patronizing discount chain stores and buying the lowest-priced food from the cheapest supermarkets. They've overlooked the fact that the products we buy and who we buy them from make a difference.

Large discount stores and franchises (whose collective size allows them to charge lower prices) are devastating small, mom-and-pop retailers, friendly and personal commercial exchanges, and Main Street economic life. Shopping at big chains and franchises concentrates money and power in fewer hands, draws cash away from the local economy, and is creating a monoculture of merchants, where every town—filled with McDonald's, 7-Elevens, Dunkin' Donuts, and Jiffy Lubes—looks the same. As for the bargain tomatoes offered at the cheapo supermarket, they are probably sprayed with pesticides and flown in from Chile, and the growers and supermarket may exploit their workers to keep prices so low.

The mistake of blindly trying to save money is most obvious with organic produce. Organic usually costs more, but a large part of that difference is because sprayers aren't picking up the tab for the environmental costs—estimated to be more than $8 billion a year in the United States alone. As someone with cheapskate inclinations, I know it can hurt to "pay up" for organic fruits and veggies, but I remind myself of two things: (1) I get frustrated with corporations for not spending a bit more to do the right thing, yet if I chose the lower-cost nonorganics, I'd be doing the same thing; and (2) the extra cost is money spent at least as well as a donation to Greenpeace. In some ways it's even better, since if everyone bought organic, there'd be one less battle for Greenpeace to fight.

If the prices of many "everyday" products included their real cleanup costs, we'd all behave differently. If gasoline, for example, reflected its true environmental expense—which the Sierra Club has estimated at $6 to $11 per gallon— Amy D.'s yard sale outings wouldn't be such a bargain.

Of course, organic foods aren't the only thing worth paying up for: there's also solar energy, electric cars, handcrafted goods, hemp products, kenaf paper, energy-efficient light-bulbs, and a good-quality bicycle, to name a just few. What these goods have in common is that they are produced by nascent industries that could really use support until they reach mass-production levels (which will lower prices); they are labor-, not energy-, intensive; or their environmental cost savings are embodied in their price. Sometimes all three are true.

What we all need to look at is how much our own consumption or "low-cost" lifestyle is impacting the earth and our own health. Are we being subsidized by exploiting either natural resources or labor? Often when something is "cheap," the answer is yes. Eliminating those subsidies means we typically need to spend more. Doing so is a willingness to add some yang—or positive, active—energy to our spending.

Like any expansion or realignment of energy, it may take time to feel comfortable with spending more for "everyday" products. Start gradually if you must. Once you see you're not going broke, you'll feel better about what you're buying.

We have the choice of surrounding ourselves with a few meaningful, healthful, and more beautiful products or—to go to the other extreme—with shoddy, impersonal, and damaging goods.

Endorsing more expensive, environmentally friendly, and humanely made products or suggesting that you buy from the mom-and-pop shop isn't a green light for spending. It's still important to ask yourself if you really need—or at least *really* want—what you're buying. What I'm advocating is a deep change in our buying habits. Instead of buying a new lawn mower, see if you can share one with a neighbor if you keep the blades sharp and/or let her use your ladder. Instead of keeping up with the latest Disney toy trend (which might be a "deal" at Kmart), use your "savings" to pay more when buying handcrafted toys. If you stick to buying the essentials and use your resources creatively, even paying more for sustainably produced goods will have the net effect of enabling you to spend less overall. Those leaner spending habits will reflect what you care about, give greater satisfaction, increase your savings, and help the environment.

What we're trying to do is find a balance—a proper alignment of yin and yang, if you will. In Buddhism there is the notion that willpower and trust are opposite faculties, which need to be balanced if we are to be healthy. We all know people who rely too much on one or the other—control freaks and daydreamers. Curbing our spending whims requires willpower; and a willingness to pay more for sustainable goods, to see your spending as an investment, takes trust. Few will achieve perfect balance, of course, but at least be aware of that goal and try to move in that direction.

If we all spent consciously, we'd have less stuff, but more contentment and a better sense of community. We may not be able to buy as much when we shop at the local hardware store instead of Wal-Mart, and that store owner would get less stuff if he bought from another local store. But at least we would all maintain greater independence and be less vulnerable to being squashed by a multinational. As with so many things, we stand and fall together.

THE FIVE CONCERNS OF HIGHLY EFFECTIVE CONSUMERS—WITH A FEW REMINDERS

Most Americans can sniff out a bargain but are blind to the nonprice issues that affect what they buy. The good news is, many nonfinancial considerations—that are good for the earth or workers or strengthen your community—are price-neutral or can actually save money. Consumer advocates estimate that shoppers are unhappy with 20 to 25 percent of their purchases. We either buy something we later realize we didn't need, end up with shoddy merchandise, or are duped by false advertising. These mistakes, in effect, act like a tax on both the planet's resources and our earnings. Researching a product and contemplating whether you really want it can reduce that levy.

At first glance, the various prepurchase suggestions in this chapter can seem like a lot to keep track of. The truth is, a thorough analysis of a product's effects can be quite complex, as many variables attend an item's manufacture, distribution, and sale. An inquiry into a "simple" T-shirt brings up pesticide use (nonorganic cotton uses more poisonous herbicides than any other crop in the world), the compensation of the factory workers, and whether the dyes used were toxic and disposed of properly. Conceivably, comparing the impact of two different T-shirts could mean making the impossible choice of deciding which is worse: endangering Canadian salmon or buying from a sweatshop manufacturer.

Fortunately, most product choices aren't so difficult. Organic T-shirt companies typically pay their workers a decent wage and don't dump their dyes into a river.

The decision process needn't be overwhelming. Knowing a few basics will usually go a long way. The fact that you're even thinking about the effects of what you buy means you're likely to consume less—and less destructively than most.

Like holistic health, conscious consumption can get complex, but like learning the gist of eating well and staying in shape, sticking to the essentials isn't hard. For both endeavors what *not* to do is just as important as what to do.

1. Habits

It's hard not to sound like a cliché when you use the phrase *paradigm shift*, but ultimately that's what is needed to transform the "American way" of consuming. More thought and greater awareness need to accompany our consumer cravings.

The Buddha taught that desires cause suffering; they also cause most shopping. Dig a little deeper. What's really behind the cravings? Are we trying to find happiness through our purchases or hoping, even subtly, to impress other people? Are you conscious of the demands and effects that come with owning lots of stuff? We may be aware of the importance of asking such questions, but how often do we actually do it at point of purchase?

When considering a new acquisition, instead of focusing

on the ways it will make you happy, mix in some healthy skepticism. For the most part, we buy something either because it's pretty or because we expect it will make life easier. Of course, there's nothing wrong with surrounding yourself with beauty, but like sumptuous food, the question is, are you overindulging? And as with food, are you looking to acquisitions as your main source of pleasure? Trying to fill yourself because something else is missing?

If we truly appreciated the enchanting things we bought, we wouldn't always be on the lookout to update or replace them. A few nice sweaters, okay, but a closetful? Likewise for shoes, dishes, and yet another love seat. By questioning the impulse to purchase, you're more likely to end up only with those things that really touch you. Think of it as good editing, which leaves a finer, if sparer, finished product.

One way to prevent excess is to avoid shopping as a recreational sport. When mall shoppers across the country were asked the primary reason for their visit, only 25 percent said they'd come for a specific item. Browsing through mail-order catalogs is also likely to create purchasing urges that otherwise would never have existed.

For practical purchases, the questions to ask are, do I really need it, will I use it a lot, and what are the alternatives? Why get a new stationary ski machine when your exercise bike still sits unused in the basement and walking, jogging, or jumping rope gives a tip-top cardiovascular workout?

When you get a hankering for something new, try putting it on a thirty-day wait list. Usually that's enough time for whims to dissipate and nudge you into finding a creative substitute. Much of what we buy we wouldn't even have thought of in the first place unless some marketer stuck it in front of us. Spaghetti cookers and popcorn makers would be some kind of a Far Side joke if millions hadn't sold. Prior to the advent of Peg-Board, nails stuck in a wall worked fine for holding hammers and screwdrivers.

Before pulling the Visa trigger, ask yourself if the item will help make you more self-reliant and involved in life or more passive and dependent. Is there an environmentally friendly alternative? And are the expense and maintenance of this item going to burden you financially or add stress to your life?

It's easy to forget that goods have needs, too. When we buy a snowblower to make clearing the driveway fast and easy, we rarely factor in the time or expense of giving it a yearly tune-up, clearing or building a good spot to store it, and keeping rust at bay. It *is* important to take care of your stuff—to make it last and truly wear it out (or give it a good home, if you realize you've made a mistake) before tossing it. Just remember that these material relationships—like all relationships—take effort and energy. Items not only need care, they also have a way of accessorizing. Snowblowers beg for a protective cover and ear protectors and neon vest for the user. Remember, if a toothbrush can engender a traveling case, anything can accessorize.

Questioning your buying motives naturally shouldn't prevent you from buying *anything*, but it can help readjust our acquisition mind-set, acting as a corrective to our normal habits.

2. PRODUCT

In general, stick with products that have multiple uses and avoid those items with highly specific purposes. One good pot can replace a rice cooker, Crock-Pot, deep fryer, and the already noted popcorn and spaghetti makers. A knife makes the cheese slicer, compact disc wrapping opener (I kid you not; millions have sold), and bagel cutter unnecessary. Even if an egg slicer costs only seventy-nine cents, why have it cluttering up your house for the two times it will really be helpful, and why add to the "unessential and pollution-creating" category of the GNP? Some items, such as the electric cookie dough dispenser, perhaps better known as "the cookie shooter," or an electric nose-hair trimmer (yes, they really exist—my gadget-happy dad has bought both) seem karmically destined to move from one garage sale to another.

Quality over quantity is a good mantra. An IKEA kitchen table costs less than a fine, handcrafted one, but when "the deal" is heading for the landfill, the craftsman's piece will be going strong with enhanced character. By the time you've bought your third, fourth, or fifth department store special, the custom-built table could be passed on as an heirloom. In the long run, the custom-built table will cost less and, more important, add integrity to your life. It will have more meaning for you while also supporting an independent artisan.

Research value and durability. This is especially important with cutting-edge technology or alternative, "breakthrough" products. Seduced by the pitch of environmental sustainability, I bought a corn-burning stove a few years ago. Unfortunately, the thing didn't give off as much heat as promised and required lots of maintenance. I should have called other stove owners before buying. (Yes, even sellers of progressive, well-intentioned products can use hype; the stove dealer eventually went out of business.) Remember the old adage: if it sounds too good to be true, check it out very skeptically.

When considering mainstream products, ask around and

then head to *Consumer Reports*. Although straitlaced and occasionally narrow-minded, *CR* usually offers fair, unbiased reviews and product comparisons. You don't even have to subscribe, since nearly every library carries it along with years of back issues. Buying reliable products should reduce repairs and prevent a quick purchase-to-junk cycle that's become so common now that many products (particularly those with electronic parts) are manufactured to be unrepairable.

Note that extended warranties or service contracts usually aren't worthwhile. Most defective products malfunction soon after initial use, when the manufacturer's own ninety-day warranty is likely to still be in effect. Retailers push extended warranties because *they* make money on them: the profit margins on warranties are sometimes twice that on the product itself—meaning the merchant may make almost as much from selling the warranty as on the original sale. It's better to pay up for a good-quality product than to attempt to buy quality through an extended warranty. The best companies will often fix any "beyond normal wear" problems on their products anyhow, even after the legal warranty expires.

When you compare prices, remember to consider not only what a quality product can replace sequentially (that is, quality costs more initially but pays in the long run) but also what it can displace *laterally* or by function. Organic raspberries may seem expensive when compared to other fruits, but when appraised as a "treat" in lieu of cake, they look reasonable (and, of course, are better for you). Similarly, a deluxe recumbent bicycle may cost a lot for a bike, but if it can replace your car, it's a deal.

3. ENVIRONMENTAL EVALUATION

Beware of books and articles that announce GREEN SHOPPING MADE EASY. For it is not. We live in a complex and interconnected world, and when you consider the full effect of your actions, few things are simple. Almost all commercial endeavors carry at least a trace of pollution. Even recycled paper consisting of 100 percent postconsumer waste is delivered in diesel-spewing trucks. This "impurity" doesn't negate our efforts; it just means most of our choices will be of the "better than" variety—and collectively that can make a real difference.

The gist of ecofriendly consuming can be summed up with the "three R's": reduce, reuse, recycle. The Green Consumer movement deserves PR kudos for getting the slogan into the national lexicon, but somehow its full intent has been lost, in that most people don't realize the R's roll off the tongue as a hierarchy—from most to least important. With all the attention recycling gets, it's easy to forget that recycling should be our last choice; it's better never to have made the garbage in the first place.

"Reducing" is best of all, of course: nothing to produce, nothing to pollute. No packaging is always better than even a recycled, biodegradable, and edible wrapping. Naturally, not everything can be reduced to nonexistence; so when possible, choose products that are efficiently made or use less energy or water to operate. Compact fluorescent lightbulbs, fans (instead of air conditioners), and water-saving toilets are "better than" alternatives.

Energy-saving choices are smart fiscally as well as environmentally: the energy savings from a new fuel-efficient hot-water heater can pay for the whole unit within a few years.

While all reducings are good, some are more crucial than

others: most notable are eliminating toxic substances such as dioxin, PCBs, mercury, benzene, and lead. These cancer-causing, fertility-threatening compounds are not only dangerous when manufactured but end up literally everywhere once released into the world. Every animal alive—from newborn babies to caribou grazing in the Arctic—has traces of dioxin and PCBs in its system.

Clearly, toxic substances should be outlawed, but until common sense wins over industry lobbying, buy only unbleached paper products and organic fruits, vegetables, and cottons. Don't use any toxic pesticides in your own home or garden; substitute biodegradable cleaners for substances like ammonia; and avoid unnecessary household chemical products such as air fresheners and toilet cleaners. While ozone-depleting chlorofluorocarbon (CFC) products are being phased out, some of CFC's substitutes, like hydrochlorofluorocarbon (HCFC), which also harm the ozone, are still on the market. Whenever possible, just say no.

"Reuse" is in some ways the neglected middle child. Often confused with recycling, reuse is actually preferable because it puts an item's full embodied energy to use. Washing and refilling milk bottles, for example, uses less energy than smashing the glass, melting it down, and reshaping it into something else.

Buying in bulk and reusing containers and grocery bags is one way to lower your shopping impact. Packaging is responsible for 75 percent of all the glass we use, 50 percent of the paper, 40 percent of the aluminum, and 30 percent of the plastic. There is an obvious irony in buying an environmentally friendly detergent in a plastic container and then not refilling it when empty (an option available in the "bulk" department at most co-ops).

There are plenty of ecomarketed "reuse" products such as rechargeable batteries or cloth diapers that may cost more initially but will save you considerably in the long run (not to mention keeping loads of leaky batteries and diapers out of the landfill). You usually don't even need to wait to reap savings when going the reuse route. Buying a used computer, for instance, is both considerably cheaper than getting a new model and better for the environment. The number of products you can buy used or refurbished is practically limitless.

While recycling is the low *R* on the totem pole, it still serves a crucial function. Turning waste products into new goods saves energy and water and reduces the impact of production. Consider motor oil: each year, the equivalent of twenty Exxon *Valdez* spills is wasted by do-it-yourselfers who either pour the used oil down the drain or throw it into the trash. Either way, it eventually results in oil contaminating our water supply—along with all the nasty by-products it picked up from the car engine, making it considerably worse than the crude that leaked into the Alaskan sound. Taking your used oil to a recycling facility or repair shop that accepts it is only the first step; the second is buying re-refined motor oil to close the loop—creating a demand for the recycled product. Bundling your newspapers doesn't make much sense, after all, unless you also buy recycled paper.

Beyond the three R's, you can further reduce your environmental wake by learning about the origin of the products you buy. Knowing how something is made can help you make better choices. For coffee to be ecofriendly, for example, it should be both harvested without pesticides *and* grown in the traditional small-farm way under the shade of a forest canopy (which provides homes for threatened songbirds as well as a myriad of other creatures).

4. THE COMPANY YOU KEEP

We've moved from a "dog-eat-dog" to a "corporate-eat-all" world. The global economy is increasingly dominated by large corporations. Of the hundred largest economies in the world (including whole countries), fifty-one are corporations. More than a quarter of the world's economic activity is carried out by the two hundred largest corporations (which employ less than one one-hundredth of 1 percent of the world's population). Exxon alone does roughly as much business as Greece and Poland combined; Mitsubishi does considerably more than Indonesia, which is the fourth most populated country in the world and loaded with natural resources.

Of course, there are good companies and bad companies— or perhaps more accurately, better and worse companies. Few large corporations can resist flexing their political clout in an attempt to slant the rules in their favor (ironically, while typically championing the power and importance of the free market). Obviously, it's better to buy from progressive, fair, and less-polluting companies. The nonprofit Council of Economic Priorities publishes guides evaluating the nonfinancial practices of large corporations.

As a general rule, products made in factories in less-developed countries are produced at the expense of the plants' workers. Without strong democratic leadership or a history of labor unions, factory workers tend to be ridiculously underpaid and subject to harsh conditions. Unless you know otherwise, assume that products from places like China, India, and Indonesia are made in dismal conditions.

As large businesses have gone global, it's become increasingly difficult for a government, a union, or an activist group to reform corporate behavior. If pushed too hard, a company may relocate—or threaten to do so. Voting with your pocket-book for responsibly made products is an important tool, especially when combined with letter-writing campaigns that inform a company of why you're ignoring its product.

When you can, try to buy products made by local artisans, small businesses, and cooperatives. Of course, there is no guarantee that the town cabinetmaker isn't a clandestine member of the John Birch Society, but after he's installed some shelves, you'll probably get a sense of what he's really like and how he runs his operation—which is more than years of transactions with Citibank would tell you. And even when the shoemaker is a creep, as one "little guy" among many, his decisions have much less influence than a large corporation's. Keeping power diffused means it's more likely to be equally shared.

Be aware that the "big boys" (and such companies are mostly run by boys) are getting hip to the fact that a certain segment of the market likes doing business with small companies. If you don't read labels carefully, you may assume from its homey packaging that the herbal tea you're buying is owned by some friendly locals when it's actually made by Kraft (which is owned by Philip Morris).

While small is often beautiful, be aware that sometimes going with the big, specialized manufacturer is the environmentally friendly thing to do—particularly with energy-efficient building materials. The energy savings of a product like Low-E windows, which will save energy for decades, justify favoring the better product over the local one. Sometimes the large, centralized plant can also make more efficient use of raw materials, have better pollution controls, and generate by-products in sufficient quantity to justify investment in symbiotic industries that utilize the waste. Even if that factory is far away, if the materials are transported mostly by rail or ship, the hauling process will be only marginally more polluting than for a regionally produced product hauled by a small diesel truck.

5. THE STOREKEEPER

Retailing is being taken over by large businesses in the form of superstores and franchises—operations that have significant advantages in buying power, resources, and efficiency. Savings are reaped from both size and ability to use a cookie-cutter template for most stores. In 1995 a new McDonald's opened somewhere on the earth every seventeen hours. Since then the rate has increased to a new Mickey Dees every three hours—or 2,500 to 3,000 new "restaurants" a year. Of course, it's not just the ghost of Ray Kroc spooking us; there's also Burger King, Wendy's, Kentucky Fried, Starbucks, and a plethora of other chains in everything from pharmacies to sporting equipment.

Given the magnitude of our global problems, I suppose a characterless, antiseptic commercial Levittown across the nation isn't the worst of our woes, but lamenting the franchising of America is more than a concern of aesthetics. Any concentration of economic power leads to a concentration of power, period. Like any elite rulers throughout history, corporate heads who manage from afar are likely to be out of touch with the needs of the communities they serve. It's difficult to trace the exact flow of dollars spent, but estimates are that for every dollar you spend at Wal-Mart, only twenty cents stay in town.

A dearth of independent stores also threatens to cut off the flow of alternative information and community news. Large chains usually restrict the posting of local notices and worry that alternative publications will offend their patrons (or corporate philosophy). As the media are consolidated into fewer hands, the importance of alternative outlets of information increases. (Twenty corporations control more than half of all U.S. media, and 80 percent of all daily papers are owned by corporate chains. Fifty years ago, 80 percent were independently owned.) If Barnes & Noble's superstores drive the small, independent bookseller out of business, who will sell a controversial book (like *The Satanic Verses*) if there's political pressure not to? How will information that questions corporate behavior find its way to the public? Even the supposedly egalitarian Internet requires marketing muscle to get heard through all the noise.

Try to avoid stores and restaurants that have more than one outlet. Obviously, this can be difficult when you pull off the highway and your choices are limited. It can also be trying when there is a big disparity in pricing. When a drill at Kmart costs ten dollars less than the one at your local hardware store, it's tempting to say to yourself, "I can save more money by buying the drill at Kmart and giving the difference to charity than by sticking with the local merchant."

If you truly gave the savings away as a donation, I suppose you'd have a point, but will you really? If it's just a rationalization (or even if it's not), why not approach the local hardware store manager and explain your dilemma: you prefer doing business with the local store and will if it can match the price. Most managers will be responsive. Even if they just narrow the price difference, the few extra bucks are worth swallowing to keep the business local.

SOME REMINDERS

Of course, rules can never substitute for good judgment and thoughtful attention to each situation as it arises. While it's important to be conscious of the what, where, and why of spending your money, as the effects are real and significant, those with zealot tendencies (such as myself) can sometimes forget that to be alive is to consume. There's no reason to feel like slime for the occasional inorganic cup of coffee at a diner or inorganic flowers picked up to surprise Mom. Guidelines are just that; keep them in mind, but don't make them your master.

Work with where you are. Take a two-ends-against-the-middle approach: focus on the easiest and hardest changes. There are plenty of little things you can do that will barely inconvenience you but make a big difference collectively—things like turning off the lights when you leave the room, lowering the thermostat at night (get an automatic one if getting out of bed on cold mornings feels like a hardship), and bringing a reusable bag for grocery shopping. It's easy to install a low-flow showerhead; hard to give up showering. So don't beat yourself up for getting clean.

As to the major lifestyle changes, target them one at a time. Trading in your gas-guzzler for a fuel-efficient car or mostly biking and taking public transit is a significant change, but one you may not be able to make right away. Eliminating beef from your diet can help reduce the harmful impact of cattle ranching. But if you're a real meat lover, it's understandable if you don't go cold turkey (meanwhile, stick to warm organic beef and turkey).

No doubt you'll sometimes be frustrated by having what seem like restrictions put on your freedom or from feeling guilty. When that happens, try to remember: First, most of us still have many more choices than our ancestors did and most of the world still does. Second, we're being *forced* to give up much more significant freedoms (such as wilderness and close-knit communities) exactly because we haven't been more thoughtful in our choices. The restrictions we're annoyed by are pretty minor compared to what will happen if we don't alter our course.

Last, don't get caught up in the blaming game. Environmentalists have often debated what is *the* most important thing to change to help the planet, focusing blame on either the individual, corporations, or government. To some extent these arguments miss the point: the gap between a sustainable, humane economy and how things are now is so great, we need progress on *all* fronts.

OUR MAJOR EXPENSES

HOME ECONOMICS: MANAGING YOUR BIGGEST PURCHASE

As my grandmother once said, "Everybody's got to be someplace." And that place, over a lifetime, is likely to cost more than anything else you buy. Why not be thoughtful about the hundreds of thousands of dollars you put toward housing?

Unless you have one of those rent-control bargains that makes you the envy of cocktail parties, in the long run, owning makes more financial sense than renting. Rents tend to rise with inflation and leave you with no equity for your efforts. Mortgage costs remain the same (or roughly so if you have an adjustable mortgage), and paying off the mortgage works as a "forced" savings plan.

And of course, owning your own home also has intangible benefits: it creates a greater sense of place and commitment to your area and community. Owning your own place gives you more control over the environmental impact your property makes (or doesn't).

Before rushing into anything, take your sense of place seriously. Know your area well before buying. Doing it right the first time will save you stress and plenty of *dinero*—since buying and selling a house is expensive. Remember, the old real estate saying "location, location, location" still holds true. After all, while you can always renovate a house, you can't move it.

There's tons of advice out there on the home-buying and -building process, so this isn't the place to repeat what can be found in more detail elsewhere. What's rarely mentioned, however, is the importance of disengaging your ego from the house hunt. Don't fall for that outdated eighties real estate industry booster, "Buy as much house as you can afford." Stretching for a house is stressful. A modest house has its advantages.

In addition to the lower initial cost, you pay less in taxes and insurance for a smaller house. And smaller homes need less fuel, repairs, and effort to maintain. The Rocky Mountain Institute estimates that most homes cost sixty to ninety cents per square foot for utilities. Living in 1,400 square feet instead of 2,200 means about an extra $600 (after tax) in your pocket each year. A basic, pleasant house is also easier to sell than a luxury model, since there are more potential buyers.

FINANCING (AND REFINANCING) FINESSE

Ideally, housing costs should be no more than 25 percent of your monthly earnings. As home prices have gone up, many families are managing at 30 to 36 percent, but before biting that much off, think about your priorities. Will higher payments mean taking on another job, giving up afternoons with your kids, or less vacation time? These questions may seem obvious now but can easily be forgotten in the heat of house hunting.

When you're ready for a mortgage, try to use either a socially concerned bank, a credit union, or a local savings and loan. A bank's lending practices and mission can strengthen your area and assist worthwhile projects or contribute to thoughtless and harmful ones. If one of these preferred sources is more expensive than a money-centered bank, tell one of its representatives your problem: you want to do business with it but need a better rate. Often your preferred source will match the competition or at least come close.

The big financial decisions when you need a mortgage are, fixed or variable, and fifteen or thirty years? Variable or adjustable-rate mortgages (ARMs) come in many flavors and varieties. A typical ARM starts with a lower interest rate than a fixed mortgage (where the rate you get is locked in for the life of the mortgage), but after the first year, the ARM adjusts according to the fluctuation of interest rates. Your new rate could be higher or lower than what you started with, capped by one-year and over-the-lifetime-of-the-loan limits (those maximums are usually two percentage points per year and six points over the life of the mortgage).

There is no definitive answer to which loan is better financially unless you can predict the direction of interest rates with *certainty* (and if you truly can, consider setting up shop as a Wall Street soothsayer). Be aware, however, that even if interest rates stay flat, the rate you pay on your ARM will go up, as banks set the first-year rate at an attractive "sign on up" discount from the Treasury index it is usually based on. Calculate for yourself what the rate would be today when that come-on discount evaporates.

As a general rule, stick to a fixed-rate mortgage. There are enough surprises and challenges in life that you don't need the added stress of finding out the roof over your head is going to cost an extra $250 or $500 a month. Since fixed-rate mortgages have a little higher rate, this means you can afford slightly less house, but at least you know you can meet your monthly nut without sweating. The uncertainty factor with an adjustable loan is reduced, of course, if you don't plan to own your house for more than five years. Then an ARM is likely to save you money, without throwing a payment monkey wrench at you.

Should mortgage rates drop after you've locked in a fixed-rate loan, you can always refinance. Don't sweat every little Fed adjustment, annoyed that you didn't get that lower rate. Small drops won't make much of a difference. To decide whether it's worth your while to refinance, figure out how long it will take reduced loan payments to recoup the bank's refinancing charges (and any possible prepayment penalties on your old mortgage). If it's less than five to seven years and you still expect to be living where you are, then go for it.

Let's say that you can lower your monthly payments $100. That means in twenty months you'll get back the $2,000 you spent in closing fees. Note, however, that if you deduct your mortgage payments on Schedule A, it will actually take longer. For an itemizer in the 28 percent bracket, $100 a month is really only worth $72 (a fact your eager mortgage lender is unlikely to point out). Sometimes in slow housing markets, banks and finance companies waive their fees for refinancing and you come out ahead immediately.

As to which is better, a thirty- or fifteen-year mortgage, stick with the fifteen-year one if you can swing it. A fifteen-year mortgage has two advantages: banks charge a slightly lower interest rate, and over the life of the loan, the total interest you pay will be cut roughly in half. Naturally, monthly payments for a fifteen-year mortgage will be higher than a comparable rate for a thirty-year mortgage since you're paying back principal faster. In the long run that's good news, since it means you'll own your home outright in half the time.

Last, your loan approval should be based solely on numbers: your earnings, current loans outstanding, and past payment history. Unfortunately, that isn't always the case, as studies by the Federal Reserve show that minorities, single women, and young people are often discriminated against. Minority mortgage applicants are two to four times as likely to be turned down than whites. Discrimination can be tough to prove, because sometimes it just takes the form of unhelpful loan officers. If you feel you've been treated unfairly, stand up for your rights; find out why your loan has been rejected. For help in the process, call the U.S. Department of Housing and Urban Development's discrimination hot line at (800) 669-9777.

WHAT YOUR CAR *REALLY* COSTS—AND HOW TAKING A DIFFERENT ROUTE CAN MAKE YOU A MILLIONAIRE

No doubt you know that cars wreak havoc on the environment. A list of the auto's sins would start with air pollution, acid rain, ozone depletion, and pavement creep (or some might say, sprint) and end with groundwater contamination, waste disposal problems, trashing wilderness for oil exploration, and maintaining a military presence in the Middle East. Despite all these reports, few of us give up our cars or seriously try to reduce our driving.

Consider, then, the money angle: the *average* expected cost of owning and operating a car during one's driving lifetime is over 200,000 smackers. Americans spend more money on cars than on food or any other major expense, for that matter, except housing.

For the last ten years, new-car prices have outpaced inflation. And the costs of maintaining a car—insurance, licensing fees, and repairs—have gone up even faster than that. Learning to lower car costs will only be increasingly valuable over time.

Most of us have only a vague idea of the cumulative, real costs of car ownership. Few even register the trade-offs they are making between minor luxuries and taking an early retirement, freedom from financial worries, or the ability to contribute to nonprofit causes. Even "economy" cars cost way more than we realize.

Although the estimated $200,000 average for a lifetime of driving will naturally vary according to the car you have, don't forget that's for just one vehicle. Two- and three-car families are shelling out $400,000 and $600,000. A recent census indicates there were 1.5 registered vehicles for every household in the United States.

While cumulative car-cost totals will impress everyone but *Forbes* 400 wanna-bes, most of us will shrug off the nosebleed numbers with "I rely on my car; what can I do?" Although it's not fun to hear, the answer is: plenty. You can walk, Rollerblade, ride your bike, take public transportation, carpool, share a car with your neighbor or neighborhood, hitchhike, move closer to work, and/or telecommute. I know that's easier said than done; it's effortless to wax philosophical over the benefits of kicking the car habit, but it's hard to actually burn your registration card. Plenty of convenience stands between you and that renunciation.

If your car is a crucial link to your income, then think about the following: If both you and your partner (should you have one) took the savings you'd glean from avoiding a lifetime of car ownership and invested it in the stock market for average or even below-average returns, you'd retire multi-millionaires. If eliminating a car from your life sounds too extreme, then consider moving toward a less carful life; that is, if you own two cars, try making do with one. If you have a large car, try managing with a compact, high-mileage one, or if you own a small compact you don't use often, look into owning one collectively. (Our family shares a "second" car with our neighbor.)

In *What Your Car Really Costs*, the American Institute of Economic Research (AIER) illustrates just how great the monetary difference can be between a small hatchback and a large sedan (the numbers would be even more dramatic if the hatchback were compared to a sport utility vehicle, which costs $26,192 more to run than the sedan). A straight comparison between the fifty-year costs of driving a big car and a compact yields a $65,694 difference ($231,454–$165,760). That roughly $66,000 difference would be considerably larger if your annual savings were invested.

Assuming that the average annual differential ($1,313) in the depreciation and maintenance costs over the life of your cars were invested each year and returned 8 percent annually (historic annual returns are 10-plus percent), at the end of fifty years, the principal and interest on that investment would amount to $814,174. After forty years it would be a sizable $367,351. If the cars were traded in during the first four years (after their greatest depreciation) or if you financed, there'd be even greater savings.

ESIMATED AVERAGE COSTS OF OWNING AND OPERATING AN AUTOMOBILE IN THE UNITED STATES FOR 50 YEARS (CURRENT DOLLARS)

AUTOMOBILE TYPE

COST CATEGORY	SMALL HATCHBACK	MEDIUM- SIZED SEDAN	LARGE SEDAN	SPORT UTILITY	PASSENGER VAN
DEPRECIATION	$ 51,960	$86,400	$95,804	$102,896	$88,606
MAINTENANCE	26,250	31,500	32,250	33,750	31,500
GAS AND OIL	33,750	44,250	48,750	51,000	43,500
INSURANCE	44,800	39,100	42,800	51,350	36,100
TAXES	9,000	11,450	11,850	18,650	16,950
TOTAL	$165,760	$212,700	$231,454	$257,646	$216,656

NOTE: BASED ON 750,000 MILES OF TRAVEL OVER 50 YEARS; 12-YEAR, 100 PERCENT DEPRECIATION ON AUTOS.

SOURCE: "YOUR DRIVING COSTS," AMERICAN AUTOMOBILE ASSOCIATION, 1996. CHART REPRINTED WITH PERMISSION FROM *WHAT YOUR CAR REALLY COSTS* BY THE AMERICAN INSTITUTE FOR ECONOMIC RESEARCH IN GREAT BARRINGTON, MA.

Remember, these numbers illustrate the costs for *typical* car owners. If you're more frugal and environmentally conscious than most—that is, if you avoid borrowing or leasing; stick to used, high-mileage subcompacts; drive your car until it's no longer usable; or fully forgo car ownership—you could accumulate a hoard big enough to run for senator in a large industrial state.

To those who would consider it fanciful or impractical to

give up a "necessity" like a car, try reframing the issue in comparison to busting your arse for a raise or a promotion or taking on a part-time job (which many traditional money guides suggest for the get-aheaders of the world).

In that context, being autoly disadvantaged looks very appealing on an after-tax, per-hour basis. The added cumulative hours it takes to travel via public transportation or, say, biking (if indeed it does take longer once you factor in the hours spent in the mechanic's waiting room or sitting in traffic) can be thought of as time paid for not driving. Then those extra benefits—such as more exercise or reading on your commute—no longer seem like idealistic, leftist pep talks but smart and effective uses of time. And if your current location makes it truly impractical to let go of your car, then the money issue makes relocating to go carless not radical but financially savvy.

In this light, it's easier to see our cultural filters: if you told someone you were moving to avoid owning a car, he or she might ask if you were in cahoots with the Unabomber. But if you told that same person you were moving for a job, he or she wouldn't bat an eye—or would perhaps applaud your initiative. Yet both moves can substantially contribute to your retirement fund.

If you took the $21,000 an average new car costs (it would actually cost more if it were financed) and invested it, withdrawing cash as needed for public transportation, occasional cabs, and car rentals, you could fund all your transportation needs for the rest of your life without affecting the principal. In fact, after twenty years—even if the stock market had been weak (going by historical precedent)—you'd have more than your original $21,000. And if the stock market had matched one of its good twenty-year showings, that $21,000 would have grown to $192,150—enough to fund your kid's four-year degree. Sure, it takes initiative to do all that, but what do you think it would take to pay for (or off) any car you bought?

FOOD FINANCES

Food is the third biggest expense for the average American family, munching 14 percent of the household budget. The way we collectively spend our roughly 650 billion eating dollars each year has an enormous impact on our health, community, and environment. Even if our food-gathering instincts have been reduced to cruising the supermarket aisles, scanning for red-dot specials, we are all, as Wendell Berry put it, "connected to the land by our gastrointestinal tract."

Food *quality* is not the place to cut corners. To lower your eating bill, buy in bulk; grow some herbs, fruits, and veggies yourself; cut back on prepackaged, processed, convenience products; lay off takeout; and ease up on restaurant outings. But don't shirk on organics—despite their generally higher cost.

I assume you know that organic produce, which avoids chemical pesticides, is healthier for body and planet. But there are a few things you may not know. First, washing chemically sprayed produce usually doesn't eliminate pesticide residues. According to a 1991 study, 85 percent of the nonleafy, nonorganic produce sold is waxed (often so lightly it's difficult to detect)—effectively sealing pesticides in.

Second, buying organic meat and dairy products is just as important as purchasing organic fruits and vegetables, if not more important, since antibiotics, drugs, chemicals, and toxins concentrate in an animal's fat.

Third, organic farms use 70 percent less energy than conventional, industrial cultivation, and if pesticides and fossil fuels were priced to reflect even a portion of their true expense to our health and the environment, "regular" tomatoes would make organics look cheap. Industrial farms are responsible for topsoil erosion, soil abuse, groundwater contamination, hazardous runoff, draining aquifers, and poisoning workers. Every time you pay a little more for sustainably produced products, you're contributing a lot to everyone's health.

Last, organic farms tend to be small, family-run operations—an increasingly rare breed. Buying organic products keeps money circulating within humane enterprises and away from large multinationals, adding character, self-sufficiency, and economic diversity to communities.

THE CASE FOR FOOD CO-OPS

Most retail, consumer food cooperatives trace their roots to buying clubs started in the late sixties and early seventies by counterculture sorts seeking healthy food. Group buying saved money and provided selection otherwise unavailable in supermarkets. By purchasing large orders directly from grocery or natural-foods wholesalers and then splitting them into family-sized portions, members saved on both labor and retail costs.

As healthy eating headed mainstream, many of these loosely structured, nonprofit associations (which often operated out of members' garages) turned into retail stores open to the public. Full-time staff usually replaced, or supplemented, member labor—although members remained the owners. (At most co-ops, when you work a certain minimum number of hours, you get discounts when you shop.)

Even after co-ops switched to professional management, they often remained informal and collectively run. For the most part, the laid-back attitude didn't hurt: co-ops thrived, unencumbered by any real competition. That retail environment has changed, however.

The 15 percent annual growth of the natural-foods business hasn't gone unnoticed by entrepreneurial shrewdies and other sophisticates with investable cash. Although traditional supermarkets have just stuck their toe into the health-food and organic scene, chains of natural-food supermarkets are muscling in—often outmarketing co-ops. In some sense, food cooperatives are victims of their own success as stores such as Bread & Circus and Mrs. Gooch's look to locate their businesses where co-ops are thriving—sometimes hiring away experienced co-op staff at salaries their small operation can't match.

While the public's greater exposure to organics and health food is good, the threat to co-ops isn't. Michael Colby, executive director of the nonprofit advocacy group Food and Water, argues that "upscale health-food supermarkets . . . do more damage than good, since they act as predators toward successful, locally based, and nonprofit food cooperatives and farmers' markets." Colby, whose organization has fought vigorously to raise awareness on food irradiation and bovine growth hormone issues, finds that natural-foods supermarkets shy away from involvement with aggressive grassroots activism. Colby also notes significant differences between how co-ops and supermarkets support local growers.

Most food co-ops are teeming with alternative publications and community notices that inform shoppers of everything from deep-ecology workshops to warnings against the dangers of biotechnologists' tampering with crops. Cooperatives often sponsor events that have nothing to do with making a profit. In some cases, in the spirit of community involvement, they may even lose sales. The Brattleboro Food Co-op, for instance, lets local organic farmers practicing community-supported agriculture (see the next subsection) use its parking lot.

Even if corporate supermarkets fully supported local organic growers and were open to alternative news, it's still preferable to shop at co-ops because they are member-owned and democratically controlled. The power and decision making, which are typically concentrated at the top in the corporate structure, are spread among all the members of a co-op. This keeps compensation of management and workers considerably more equitable than for most corporations. The profits of a co-op benefit all the owners of the co-op as opposed to mainly going to stockholders.

COMMUNITY-SUPPORTED AGRICULTURE: GIVING "SHARECROPPING" A NEW MEANING

Every year 400,000 acres of prime farmland are lost to development—pastures and fields turned into subdivisions, strip malls, condos, office parks, and roads. One way to keep small farms alive, while also getting a good deal on healthy produce, is to buy your fruits and veggies directly from the farmer. You can do this at farmers' markets or through a community-supported agriculture, or CSA, partnership.

Although the formula for how each CSA works differs from farm to farm, the basic gig is, before the growing season starts, you pay anywhere from $200 to $400 for a share of the harvest. Some CSAs require you to work a minimum number of hours; others make labor optional and even deliver your tomatoes, bok choy, and kale to your doorstep.

CSA subscribers usually find they've gotten a bargain, receiving far more produce than their few hundred dollars would buy in the store. While there is always the possibility of blight or drought hurting your crops—as a subscriber, you share the good and the bad with the farmer—most say they get so much produce they have to share it with neighbors. (Some CSAs offer half subscriptions.)

Most CSAs are organic, and some are biodynamic—which means they follow some principles of sustainable farming and nature as defined by Rudolf Steiner.

SPENDING TAI CHI

BOYCOTT POWER AND HOW TO WIELD IT

After biking home from work, eating an organic salad for dinner, and sending off your annual dues to Greenpeace, you decide to kick back with an ice-cold Kirin Beer—not realizing you're supporting Mitsubishi, destroyer of rain forests. No, don't make that a Bud, since Friends of Animals is calling for Anheuser-Busch/Sea World to release an orca unnecessarily kept in captivity. Welcome to the world of consumer boycotts.

While product sensitivity is easy pickings for David Letterman parodies of political correctness, the truth is, once you know about a boycott, it is pretty simple to follow. And the good news is, when boycotts are well organized, they really work. After all, they hit a corporation where it matters most: its pocketbook.

Economic boycotts have a long and illustrious history, tracing their lineage from the American colonies' Stamp Act in 1765 to Martin Luther King Jr.'s call to stay off Alabama buses to the Earth Island Institute's campaign against tuna fishing that killed dolphins.

A nationwide survey of business executives indicated that

they consider boycotts more effective than class-action suits, lobbying, and stand-alone letter-writing campaigns. Companies hate the loss of sales and negative publicity boycotts bring—an image problem that can dog them for decades, even after they've reformed. They also know that the consumers who are most likely to heed a boycott—namely, the college-educated, thirty- to fiftysomething, double-income family crowd—are exactly whom marketers want to win over.

The downside to the success of boycotts is that there are now so many out there, it's often hard to remember who's to be avoided and why. Levi Strauss, for example, which is generally considered one of the hipper and more benevolent bastions of capitalism, is being boycotted by La Fuerza Unida for the company's refusal to give full compensation to San Antonio, Texas, workers when it moved a factory to Costa Rica.

As with anything else, you have to pick and choose your fights. Better to follow a few boycotts well—encouraging friends, writing letters, and posting notices in your co-op—against companies that really upset you than vaguely pursue a bunch. It can take years before a boycott has an effect. Most companies won't even realize there's a boycott against them unless it is a well-organized and publicized action orchestrated by an established group.

It's crucial to accompany any refusal to buy a product with a letter to the company explaining why. As Rob Callahan, organizer of the Boycott Board—a Web site that indexes, summarizes, and gives links to progressive boycotts—points out, "Chances are, Disney isn't likely to notice your $7 missing from the millions it rakes in at the box office. And even if it does, how will the company know a decline in sales is attributable to outrage over the treatment of labor in Haiti?"

The most effective boycotts typically have one or more organizations promoting them. That multiplies the loss of $7 ticket sales a thousand- or millionfold. INFACT's boycott against GE accounted for approximately $60 million in lost revenue—an attention-getting number, even for a multibillion-dollar corporate behemoth.

THE PLASTIC PARADOX: CREDIT CARDS THAT GIVE BACK

Gone are the days when a "card-carrying environmentalist" denoted someone who pays Greenpeace membership dues. Now it's just as likely to describe someone with a credit card—issued in the name of the Sierra Club, Wilderness Society, or any of a growing number of environmental groups looking for a piece of the action in plastics.

What's drawing these groups to affiliate with credit card–issuing banks is the fees such cards generate. With donations stagnant, it's hard to resist tapping into the lucrative resource of a large membership. As any direct marketer can tell you, numbers pay.

Even if only a small percentage of the Sierra Club's 500,000 members become Sierra credit card holders, and even if the club receives only .5 percent of every transaction those cardholders make, that still adds up to some serious cash. The Wilderness Society's nearly 15,000 cardholders added $200,000 to its operating budget in 1995. During the first ten years in which credit cards were issued in the Sierra Club's name, its 55,000 credit card–wielding members contributed nearly $2 million to the organization's bottom line. That money translates into more environmental protection.

Of course, all this environmental plastic isn't without its irony. Charge cards are the grease that keeps the consumer society rolling—wreaking havoc on the environment. To misquote Ross Perot, that sucking sound you hear each time you whip out your credit card is the sound of natural resources being converted into products.

Critics, including Ralph Nader, point out that environmental credit cards help legitimize wanton consumption. Nader objects to "the serious institutional pathology of credit-card issuers who encourage consumers to pile up debt." He points out that credit cards raise prices for everyone who pays in cash and make invasions of privacy possible through computerized compilation of consumer spending patterns. Nader himself refuses to own a credit card.

But then again, when your face is too famous to qualify for an American Express "Do-you-know-who-I-am?" commercial, you don't need one. Nader's staff, for example, makes plane reservations for him. Most of us, however, need credit cards at least sometimes and thus still face the question of which one to use. Why not use one that contributes to causes you support?

The original socially responsible credit card was started by Working Assets in 1986. Transaction fees from Working Assets support a wide array of good causes—from Children's Defense Fund to Friends of the Earth. Cardholders vote annually to determine which groups to support. In 1995 Working Assets contributed $2.1 million to thirty-six groups. There is no yearly fee for the card, and each time you use it, ten cents is added to Working Assets' donation pool.

The typical deal for cards sponsored by nonprofits is, no annual fee and low annual financing rates on unpaid balances for the first five months (after that, as with most cards, interest charges rise to the stratosphere). The affiliated nonprofits typically receive $3 for each new cardholder, $5 for each yearly renewal, and .5 to 1 percent of each billed transaction.

If your average Visa purchase is more than $20, then one of these cards will help nonprofits more than Working Assets (since it donates 10 cents per transaction regardless of purchase size). If you are undecided about which group you want to support, ask exactly what percentage of your purchases will be donated to your favorite organizations and go with the highest nonprofit fee generator. You'll need to ask the groups themselves, as the banks that finance the credit cards won't say.

One last option, offered with the caution of "Don't try this at home unless you are truly disciplined," is to get a cash-back card such as GE Rewards (yes, as in General Electric). Depending on how much you charge, the GE Rewards card annually rebates .5 to 2 percent of your purchases, with a cap of $140 per year.

In theory, a couple charging $20,000 a year on two separate cards could generate a $280 check to be donated to the charity of their choice—with practically no effort. Standing in the way of that donation will be an onslaught of coupons from GE and affiliated corporate "partners," enticing you to spend your "free" cash. There is also, of course, the irony of doing business with one of America's largest polluters to create charitable giving. For some, that irony is sweet.

A DOZEN WAYS TO WARD OFF THE
COMMERCIAL ONSLAUGHT

About the only way to totally escape commercialism in the United States is to head for the woods. Even then, you're likely to come across a hiker with a big Nike logo emblazoned across his chest or see a small plane skywriting for a car dealer. So rather than seek the impossible—an absence of advertising and PR noise—which would only drive you mad, aim for some shelter from the marketing storm.

Like the fish oblivious to water, most of us don't realize the influence commercial messages have on us. We're so surrounded by ad pitches that they seem an inevitable part of life. But once you free up a little brain space—the ultimate place advertisers are targeting—you'll appreciate just how noisy it's been.

Here are some suggestions to counteract the marketing attack:

1. Be Prepared. By increasing one's awareness of how ubiquitous commercialism is, one is less prone to buy it. Remembering a marketer's main weapon—creating dissatisfaction (and then showing how the marketer's item will remedy it)—makes it less likely we'll fall for the pitch.

2. The Obvious: Cut Back the Tube. If it were up to me, television would be illegal—or at least regulated (there are more TV addicts in this country than alcoholics, and television is toxic to clear thinking and intelligent public debate). Since we all know how likely that is to happen, it's up to you to cut back if you want to minimize the effect of the world's most powerful advertising medium. If you don't want to give up your favorite shows, then at least tape them and bypass the commercials when you watch.

Curbing the TV habit can even have a tangible payoff: Harvard economist Juliet Schor found that the more television a person watches, the less money she saves. Controlling for age, income, and other demographics, Schor estimates that each hour of television viewing per week reduces your annual savings by $208.

3. Protect Your Children. Children are highly susceptible to advertising, which inspires a whining for goodies and, even worse, the repetitive parroting of catchy slogans and jingles, literally ad nauseam. Curbing the TV will go a far way here. Put it in the closet and only wheel it out when something special is on.

Take a stand against advertising in schools, particularly "news" programs like Whittle's Channel One, which are primarily vehicles for corporate messages. Encourage schools to offer media literacy courses, so children can think intelligently about what they're exposed to. (How many kids, let alone grownups, know that roughly 85 percent of the news they read is inspired by public relations campaigns?)

4. Just Say No to Logos. The plain T-shirt or cap has become a rare breed. Why buy something that sells someone else's stuff? Even if you get it as a freebie, if you don't support the message, why wear it? Using a Coca-Cola towel burns its image ever so slightly deeper into our gray matter.

Since Wall Street discovered that enduring brand names are more valuable than labor, factories, or patents, corporations are working more feverishly than ever to make their mark stand out. It's easy enough to remove the "Intel Inside" sticker from your PC or cover the "Panasonic" name on your answering machine so at least your home is logo-free.

5. Buy with Cash. When you pay with a credit card or use your supermarket discount card, your purchase gets recorded somewhere in the marketing database universe, creating a consumer profile, which gives businesses or anyone else with greenbacks access to your particular tastes. Cash leaves no trace.

6. Refuse to Fill Out Surveys. You don't need to fill out a questionnaire to get a product warranty. The information you give the company only pads its data banks.

7. Stay Away from Malls and Chain Stores. Fast-food places and other franchises often do cross-marketing. McDonald's gives away Disney figures. At Sony theaters you get vouchers for Burger King. Large corporations feel comfortable doing business with and promoting other large corporations.

8. Make Your Voice Heard. When a movie theater puts advertising before the feature film, complain to the manager (reminding her that for every one complaint she hears, there are twenty-four others who feel the same way but haven't said anything to her).

Ask your political representatives to ban billboard advertising, as Alaska, Hawaii, Maine, and Vermont have (though note that you're up against an industry that pumped $500,000 into the 1996 congressional election coffers). And while you've got your political pen out, lobby for increased funding of commercial-free arts and media and restrictions

on using information gleaned from consumer spending
habits.

To go on the offensive, support the Media Foundation, publisher of *Adbusters Quarterly* (www.adbusters.org),
or other guerrilla media counterpunchers that disseminate
parodies of ads. One "culture-jamming" group, the Barbie
Liberation Organization, bought hundreds of Barbie and
G.I. Joe dolls, altered them by switching their sound chips,
and then, in a reverse-shoplifting move, put them back on
store shelves. The new, macho Barbies bellowed, "Vengeance
is mine," while Joe intoned, "Let's go shopping."

Simpler protests can be voiced by using the postage-paid
envelopes junk mailers sent (sans order, of course) to voice
complaints.

9. Reduce or Eliminate Junk Mail. Totally abolishing your
share of the 65 billion pieces of junk mail that are sent each
year is a job for a dedicated environmentalist only. It would
require contacting all the major list brokers, credit bureaus,
and government agencies, such as the department of motor
vehicles, that rent out names and asking them to leave you
alone. Then you would need to get in touch with all the
magazines, active credit cards, and mail-order catalogs you
do wish to receive and request that your name stay on their
"in-house-only" list.

A quicker, easier method, which will slow but not kill the
junk-mail flow, is to contact the Mail Preference Service of
the Direct Marketing Association (P.O. Box 9008, Farming-
dale, NY 11735; [212] 768-7277) and ask it to remove your
name. Your name and address will be put on DMA's "Delete
File," which is supposedly used by most of its 3,600-plus

members. This list is sent out four times a year, so it could take three months before it affects your mailings. The tricky part is making sure the DMA has your name and address in all the various ways it appears on the junk mail you get.

Your name will stay on the "delete" rolls for five years, but even that will be short-circuited if you order something via mail and don't request to stay on the in-house-only list.

10. Tame Telemarketers. Reducing telemarketing calls is similar to cutting down junk mail. The first step is to contact the Telemarketing Preference Service, which is operated by the Direct Marketing Association, and ask to be removed from calling lists.

After that, you need to take a case-by-case defense. Federal law requires telemarketers to ax your name from their lists and never call you again if you request it. Record the names, addresses, and the dates of your requests and file a complaint with the Federal Trade and/or Federal Communications Commission if your demand isn't heeded.

Further federal regulations on telemarketing state:

- You should never get a call before eight A.M. or after nine P.M.
- Unsolicited faxes are illegal.
- A prerecorded machine-delivered message must disconnect you within five seconds after you hang up.

For those who want to take the "easy" way out and feel uncomfortable slam-dunking on unsolicited callers, it's usually easy to sidestep telemarketers by remembering that anyone who asks for you by "Mr.," "Mrs.," or "Ms." is trying to sell you something. That's your cue to ask, "Who's calling?" and then let the AT&T representative know you've permanently moved to Madagascar to lay lines for MCI (or vice versa, of course, if MCI is calling).

Naturally, there's always call screening for those who have an answering machine or, if you're really besieged, caller ID. Last, if you're in a feisty mood, ask the telemarketer for his home number so you can call him back later.

11. Spurn Spam. Anyone who has an E-mail address knows she is subject to random solicitations promising a more financially dynamic, charismatic, longer, easier, odor-free, and less-expensive life (in cyberlingo such junk mail is known as "spam"). Junk E-mail wastes our time, collectively ties up phone lines, and undermines the original helpful culture of the Net. If you want to keep these annoying messages out of your face, there are a few things you can do.

First, be careful about where you sign your E-mail address. Many Web sites exist to generate "mailing" lists, which are sold to spammers. Other marketers cull addresses from user groups. The more you put your "signature" out there, the more likely you are to get spammed.

Second, consider registering your desire to opt out of junk E-mail at Netiquette.Net (www.junkbusters.com). As with DMA delete lists, the hope is that responsible spammers will remove anyone from their files who has officially objected.

Third, complain, complain, complain. It's annoying to have to even respond, but ultimately, spammers will only stop if their results aren't worth the hassle. Sometimes protesting to the spammer's server can be effective. If the mailer's real address is disguised, you can get its phone number and address by pretending you're interested in what it's offering. Then call the mailer up and gripe directly. Some hackers fight spammers by "bombing" them (returning the junk E-mail hundreds of times or sending huge files that clog or disable the receiver's mailbox), but these guerrilla tactics are of questionable legality and could start an E-mail war.

12. Put Cookies on a Diet. For those unfamiliar with cyberlingo, "cookies" are small text files that a Web site can attach to your computer equipment to glean information about what your buying habits and Internet browsing patterns are. If this sounds spooky, that's because it is. Internet browsers (like Netscape) can be programmed to block cookies or alert you when they come up. This can sometimes be inconvenient or make certain sites inaccessible. If you want to surf the Net without total anonymity and not have to mess with cookies, there are several software programs that allow you to do so. (See the appendix for your options.)

EARNING IT

LOOKING FOR AN INSIDE JOB

"How we spend our days is, of course, how we spend our lives," wrote Annie Dillard. And most of us spend those days working. Our occupation literally occupies us, determining how we will feel when we wake up each morning and return home each evening. No interaction with money has a greater impact on our daily lives than what we do for pay.

Most money guides, however, give short shrift to our working life. Or they tell you about the hottest job prospects for the decade ahead. The assumption seems to be, it doesn't so much matter how you get the dough, just amass as much as you can. The bottom line has been moved to the top, squashing the heart of the matter: finding work that is engaging and meaningful, that allows creative expression and leaves room for a life outside the job.

Considered historically or globally, having a choice to work for love or money is a privilege. The price of that freedom is that it puts many of us on the horns of a dilemma: Do we trust our heart and cosmic forces or play it safe? Do we take the beaten path or follow our own muse? And beyond that big choice lie countless shades of alternatives: Just how much creativity are we willing to sacrifice in the name of salary? When does compromise make sense? And if it does, what's the best way to swing it?

Studies show that most people dislike their job; roughly 80 percent wish they were doing something else. It's hardly surprising, then, that more heart attacks happen between eight and nine on Monday morning than any other time.

If you're dissatisfied with your work, no one has to tell you that you should make changes. But you may want some direction and confidence to know you're on the right path or, if you've found something you think you like, some inspiration to stick with it when doubts creep in. Most career guides have you assess yourself to see where you can fit in. A better approach is to work from the inside out: mine your own interests, talents, and values to determine what work will fit you. This may not land you a new-millennium kind of job, but it will help you find work you can feel passionate about—no matter what's happening in the economy. That will give you a true bang from your bucks.

GROPING THROUGH THE WORK MUDDLE

Job seekers are swamped by information, choice, and uncertainty, tinged with ominous foreshadowing. Large corporations continue to command more power while offering employees less security. Technology and the economy are changing so quickly, even those at the cutting edge aren't sure how to play the future. It's hard to know where we'll fit in. And as if that weren't enough, we're filled with conflicting emotions about work: part of us wants to express ourselves creatively; part desires success via money, power, and recognition; part wishes to heed our altruistic impulses; part seeks security (when not called by the excitement of risk); and part longs for some breathing room. We want satisfying, meaningful work, plenty of dough, and a balanced life. In short, we want it all. Needless to say, that's a tall order.

It's not that the good life—or more accurately, *a* good life—isn't possible, but it is likely to take a different form from what we imagine. Don't figure on slipping into the perfect, compromise job that satisfies all these urges at once—unless perhaps you have towering talent and smarts to spare. Rather, "solutions" are likely to come from a combination of changing how we feel about money and success, taking a different approach to how we organize our work life, and bringing greater awareness and acceptance to our myriad desires and the tension they create. Most attempts to mix inspiration, purity of purpose, and money will be balancing acts. The question is, can you manage it with your eyes and heart open—making the journey and its perils part of living adventurously?

In your fantasies you may see yourself dashing off an incisive piece of investigative journalism for *The New Yorker*, just in time to greet the kids stepping off the bus. Or you might picture your new Internet business (managed in between traveling, working on your photography, and a rigorous fitness regimen) receiving national coverage. But to pull those off—or even considerably less glamorous versions of those— takes both serious chops and plenty of toil. Somehow we tend to forget that and instead imagine that our problem is, we're not working hard or smart enough. The clock becomes a relentless, mocking taskmaster.

The first thing to look at is what's behind grand fantasies. Of course, wanting success, respect, or recognition is natural, but larger-than-life fantasies (and their often accompanying drive) beg investigation. Desires for fame, power, or wealth are frequently propelled by unresolved emotional needs. Who are we really trying to impress and be accepted by, and why? What hurt or longing are we hoping to redress? Releasing yourself from mondo expectations can ease the way for greater satisfaction from the work you're doing now and allow you to pursue something that is truly appropriate for you. Besides, as most everyone knows—if not firsthand, then from reading celebrity bios—fame and money per se don't bring real fulfillment. There's always another pinnacle to conquer, since these trophies are substitutes for what we're really after (for most of us, acceptance and love).

Since we can't have it all, we must make choices. But our choices aren't necessarily between all or nothing. Consider nontraditional, surfing-your-situation approaches to work that offer flexibility. For example, instead of trying to write the *New Yorker* profile before playing with the kids, consider putting them in more day care (or afternoons with friends) for a couple of weeks and then spend more time than usual with them after deadline. This can reduce the distracting splitting that comes when your mind is managing two tasks at once.

This approach can work in a larger time frame, too. Right now it may be awkward for you to practice your craft or follow your muse—especially if it doesn't pay well (as is often the case with creative and altruistic work). If there are pressing matters to tend to and bills to pay, then realism should be the better part of valor. Sure, if it weren't for strong coffee and $35 per hour, you'd never proofread legal textbooks. But if putting in just a few hours a day lets you care for your elderly mom, homeschool your children, paint, meditate, garden and cook, train for the Ironman Triathlon you've dreamed about, or convalesce from an ulcer, why not? For many, having the freedom to control their lives, even if it simply means being able to go to the post office at two P.M. on a Tuesday, is more important than a career that requires serious commitment or one that pays so poorly you have to work in overdrive to get by.

Often such flexible arrangements are temporary. Scheduling for children, for example, can be altered as they grow up. Adjusting to their lives may put a crimp in your career, but one hopes this offers its own rewards and—when considered in the context of a working lifetime—is a pleasant interlude.

Learning to love what you do until you do what you love is an art, with its own challenges and compensation. Actresses and novelists waiting tables can hone their craft observing how lovers converse when they're estranged, excited, or bored. More important, you can work on appreciating life's "undramatic" moments. All situations offer fodder for the soul. Watch out when you attempt to dismiss unglamorous work. Throwing yourself into everything you do, even if it doesn't immediately grab you, helps soften the ego, builds enthusiasm for all of life, and shows a commitment to excellence. Every circumstance offers an opportunity.

Of course, acknowledging that compromise is sometimes needed doesn't mean it's ideal. Before giving up on meaningful work, consider cutting your expenses. What's often overlooked is how our spending habits burden our work life. Are cable service, regular takeout (comforts that are especially enticing when you're fried), and Aspen ski vacations worth compromising for? "Small" luxuries add up, and their real, after-tax, after-commuting cost comes out of our sweat and fret. Spend less and you can work less.

If there is little fat to trim from your budget and you must take a job mainly for its pay, try to maintain lean spending habits even after pulling in bigger bucks. This can pay off in work freedom later. While I wouldn't recommend that everyone go the route I took (that is, working as a stockbroker for a few years to stash away a chunk of savings), it has worked out reasonably well. I've been able to pursue work that interests me and that I value while maintaining a moderately comfortable lifestyle—even though the work I do now pays modestly. Savings, when invested well, can grow on their own and supplement low-paying but satisfying work for your whole lifetime. You don't need a fortune to provide acceptable independence and flexibility.

It's a mistake to seek *full* financial independence so you can do meaningful work later: for one thing, it's likely to take so long you'll get sidetracked from your original intent; for another, you'll probably never feel as if you have enough—since it's the money you're relying on, not yourself. Any savings-for-work-freedom goals are better set with the idea of establishing a crutch, not a panacea. This alternative can allow you to focus on the money part of the work pickle mostly at once, so it nags less later. Although it doesn't let you have it all, it can make things easier.

Remember also, when you earn your living from work you love, you need less money for retirement. If your work is fulfilling, you'll want to keep doing it (and will earn some income) well into your golden years. If the idea of needing to generate an income when you're older sounds scary, consider an even scarier scenario: spending your whole working life doing something you don't care about. When senior citizens are asked what they would have done differently if they could live their life over again, they consistently say they wish they'd focused more on the meaningful and been willing to take more creative risks.

My point isn't to recommend a program but to mention options that can help you wade through work/money dilemmas. The rest of Part 4 is devoted to finding and attempting to achieve an ideal work situation.

THE IDEAL: FINDING YOUR CALLING

Freud said that satisfaction in work and love are the keys to a fulfilling life. True enough, and a melding of the two is better yet. Work you feel passionate about is infused with love. It allows you to express yourself and touch others.

There is a real distinction between a job or career, which is mainly good for the paycheck, and a vocation or calling you do for the meaning—and the pay takes care of bills. Work that speaks to you gives purpose; it supplies a "why" in what can sometimes feel like a confusing and overwhelming cosmic soup. Whether this urge is fueled by a creative itch or from wanting to right a wrong, it's our ticket to making our mark, no matter how small. It means that making a living and really living aren't at odds.

Joseph Campbell, mythology scholar turned popular shaman, called the pursuit of meaningful work "following your bliss." When you do that, Campbell said, you stay at the center of the wheel of fortune, less perturbed by the cycle of ups and downs that invariably comes with any career or life. Happily, that dedication to passion produces an excellence that increases the odds of good fortune. But wealth or recognition isn't the point; you're already reaping rewards.

Discovering work that combines your purpose and passion

is a boon; actually being able to make a living from it is a blessing. Those who have struggled before finding it experience a sense of coming home—that "aha" feeling that also comes with psychological insight.

Finding your ideal work, like finding an ideal mate, may come easily, be a struggle, or never happen; but usually we don't find *the* perfect match. We're better off seeking a direction than a destination. Don't discount work that grabs you but has elements that drive you nuts. Or maybe you'll need more than one job to be happy. Getting the work thing right is likely to require some tinkering. Of course, you shouldn't limit yourself to a neat job description any more than you should have a traditional marriage if that doesn't work.

WORKING FROM THE INSIDE OUT

Live from the inside out. Unless you start with yourself—how you're built, what you value, what you like—how can you possibly find meaningful work? It seems so obvious, but after these thoughts fade, doubts and fears can pour in. Often, what's fueling these worries are concerns about the much-heralded changing economy. Not wanting to be road-kill to the shifting marketplace, we focus on how we'll fit in, not on what we need.

Don't panic. Yes, the economy is changing. Yes, you should be willing to learn new tricks and be aware of trends, but that doesn't change the fundamentals of uncovering your muse and fulfilling your core needs. Even if job particulars change, you should always be able to do the essence of your thing. Psychotherapists, for example, may see patients via videophones, or they may have to become more entrepreneurial to survive, but there will still be a place for people who work healing the psyche.

Naturally there are no guarantees: it's possible (if highly unlikely) that psychotherapists could go the way of the buggy whip. But trying to base your career choice on the latest forecasts gives no guarantees either. The economy is a moving target, and futurists are just as likely to miss the mark as you are. But when you lead with what you love, you can never fully lose. You may need new training, but the process of developing skills you care about is worthwhile in and of itself—and should be applicable in some way to anything you do.

WHAT DO YOU *REALLY* LIKE?

Rattling off a list of things that give you pleasure—*Thin Man* movies, cappuccino, and sex—is easy enough; it may even give clues to what your calling is. But more important is discovering what you find fulfilling. Fulfillment comes from a deeper place—from a mixture of doing something with integrity, living according to your values, and using your talents. Finding work that satisfies these requires listening closely to your genuine inner voice. It means culling through your swirl of emotions, expectations, adopted cultural myths, and fantasies.

Most of us engage in a kind of unruly, internal wrestling match, torn between what we really want to do and what we think we're supposed to do—often trying to avoid facing either. Pieces of our real yearnings come to us obliquely and fleetingly, as though from a dream. To hear our true wisdom requires a combination of lowering the volume of competing voices and agendas, and staying with uncomfortable feelings in a nonjudgmental way. This, as the spiritual teacher J. Krishnamurti pointed out, takes great humility: "If you start by saying, 'I know myself,' you have already stopped learning about yourself."

Part of the problem is, we just don't have—or make—the time for soul-searching. Writer and career-workshop leader Melissa Everett quotes a New York architect who speaks for many: "Sure I have time to reflect on my life," he said. "Sometimes for five minutes at a stretch, if I'm alone in a cab." Without a commitment to introspection, creating a better work life is almost impossible. Try thinking of introspection as the research and development function of You Inc. Otherwise, as with any enterprise that doesn't invest in itself, you may eventually crash and burn.

Regularly checking in with yourself by taking a little quiet time or meditating (even for five minutes) and keeping a work-related diary can be helpful. Note what sparks and holds your interest—and what doesn't. Pay attention to your work habits and how you process information. Find out what you're really like, not how you want to be. Otherwise, you may continually recreate situations that don't work for you— like the multiple-divorces fellow who marries the "same" woman again and again.

To distinguish between passion and pleasure, see if you're drawn to go beyond superficialities. How do you react when the going gets tough? Do you like studying your chosen endeavor—researching and experimenting on your own? Are you willing to sacrifice other pleasures for its pursuit? Is the activity you're drawn to engrossing and compelling? Dashing off a letter can be fun, but are you up for the discipline, research, detail, and organizing that writing a book entails? Obviously, even "born" writers get frustrated or dislike parts of the profession, but the overall process of writing must be rewarding.

Here are some exercises and thoughts to help uncover your skills and inspirations:

- Jot down *activities* that make you happy.
- What did you like as a child? Make your memories as

vivid as possible. Try to conjure up those special moments when you were alone, daydreaming or playing exactly what you wanted. Did you love machines, drawing, putting on plays, or organizing parties?

• Imagine you're at a daylong seminar that will break down into six groups of people according to broad interests and skills.

Group A: Those who are interested in working with things—machines, tools, plants, animals—and who like being outdoors. They have athletic or mechanical talents.

Group B: Number crunchers, data strokers, and good detail people who cheerfully do what is asked of them and don't necessarily need to know why. They like seeing results.

Group C: People who want to spread the word or get a message out about how to do things better. They tend to be skilled with words and storytelling.

Group D: Artistic, innovative, or intuitional sorts who like unstructured surroundings and using their creativity.

Group E: People who are adept at organizing, influencing, and performing. They tend to be entrepeneurial.

Group F: Analyzers who enjoy observing, learning, investigating, evaluating, or solving problems.

Consider which group you'd want to spend the day with. If your favorite group had no more room, which cluster would you choose next? How about if that one were filled, too? Don't think so much in terms of what you're good at but whom you like hanging out with. It can give you some idea about what might be a good work atmosphere and environment of coworkers for you.

- Even if you dislike your current job, what is it that you enjoy most about it? How about previous work? Which aspects appealed to you most?
- Explore the enneagram and Myers-Briggs personality systems.

The enneagram is a centuries-old psychological system with roots in sacred traditions. Its often trenchant insights into the nine different personality types have given it credibility among the progressive business community; the Stanford School of Business even offers an enneagram course.

The Myers-Briggs system is based on four basic aspects of personality: how we interact with the world, where we direct our energy, the kind of information we naturally notice, and how we make decisions. All the various combinations of these four elements create sixteen fundamental personality types. Understanding your type can help you more clearly see how you operate.

If you're already reasonably self-aware, these perspectives can affirm and expand what you've already suspected about yourself. This can confirm whether you're on the right career path or direct you elsewhere. Perhaps most important, they can indicate the blind spots that usually go with our personality type. Our weaknesses are often difficult for us to see and accept, yet working with those vulnerabilities is the key to fully developing (see appendix for resources).

MINING YOUR DREAMS

"If necessity is the mother of invention," notes Laurence Boldt in *Zen and the Art of Making a Living*, "then playfulness is the father." Harnessing your imagination, the mind's ability to "what if," can lead you to satisfying work. It's not that we need to make ourselves fantasize—as we could hardly stop that if we tried. Rather, we need to bring awareness to our dreams, honoring inspirations and shining light on what might otherwise remain wistful yearnings. Neglected, real cravings turn into regrets.

Creative insights are best cultivated through absorption and relaxation. Dive into the issue of your life's work. Read about it, think about it, and then let go. Inspiration can't be bullied into shape; it bubbles to the surface. Letting go of both tension and realism allows artistic insight to flourish.

Fantasizing without regard to "reality" frees you to engage in soaring aspirations and dreams, without burdensome expectations or fear of failure. Look closely at work fantasies you'd be embarrassed to share. Even if they're half-baked, they often contain important ideas. Of course, don't discount work that doesn't sound spiffy enough. If your corporate VP dad is disappointed at the idea of your becoming a carpenter, that's really, as they say, HP not YP (his problem, not your problem).

Recurring yearnings are obviously telling us something important, but sometimes we get so used to them—almost as a fixture of our semisecret self—that we stop listening. Which fantasies have stayed with you through thick and thin? I'm not talking about the desire to be a movie star, after seeing DeNiro in *Raging Bull*. But when you're walking through the woods alone or cruising down the freeway, what does your mind keep going back to? Not just this week, but over the years? Look for themes in your various fantasies; by analyzing these, you can find your core interests. Thinking about them in a systematic way can give you important information.

Notice whom you admire most or even envy. There's a reason another's life grabs you. Learn about that person and see if he or she can be a role model—or even a mentor. You may be able to work as the person's apprentice, offering to type or do paperwork in exchange for guidance. Personal-achievement gurus tell us to study those who've mastered what we're interested in. If nothing else, you'll uncover the gritty details: delivering babies, for instance, is exciting, but follow a midwife or an obstetrician around for a week and you'll feel the sacrifices in sleep and personal time you'll have to make.

EXERCISES

- Consider the $10-million question: If you had total financial security, how would you spend your time? This daydreaming helps separate out the money issue from what you like.
- Write down work fantasies. Over a period of a few months, you'll see which ones repeat. Look for recurring and dominant themes.
- Envision your funeral. What would you want your spouse, sibling(s), good friends, children, and someone who knows you from work and community efforts to say? In other words, look at how you'd like to live in the fullest sense. What does that tell you about what your goals should be?

- In *The Artist's Way*, Julia Cameron suggests we free-associate by completing the following sentences:

  If I could lighten up a bit, I'd let myself . . .
  I don't do it much, but I enjoy . . .
  If it weren't too late, I'd . . .
  If I'd had the perfect childhood, my work would be . . .
  If it didn't sound so crazy, I'd write, make, or do . . .

- Dreams give us the freedom to experiment and make unconscious connections. Before going to sleep at night, ask yourself to dream about finding your calling.
- Investigate the following fears: of poverty, of criticism, of bad health, of old age, of loss of love, and of death. Do any of them hold you back from pursuing what inspires you?
- Solitude allows us to hear what we really want without distractions. Consider going camping by yourself or attending a meditation retreat, dedicated to finding your purpose in life.

CONSIDERING THE "T" WORD: TALENT

Most career guides gloss over the issue of talent—as in, do you have enough of it to be paid to do the work you love? Since the answer is sometimes no, career-counselor authors usually sidestep the issue rather than temper their upbeat tone. But to ignore assessing your talents is to bury your head in the sand; maybe you can get away with it, but it's hardly a sound strategy.

The good news is, there's little reason to hide: most jobs,

even appealing ones, are accessible if you're willing to work hard. We may not be erudite or witty enough to be an editor at *The New York Review of Books*, but working for a local paper or magazine is within the reach of most avid readers who learn to polish their prose.

The even better news is, our talents usually correspond to what we're drawn to. Research on child prodigies indicates they burn to express their gift. Psychologist Abraham Maslow, of self-actualization fame, found that the talents we're born with eventually surface as a need—and deserve our attention.

Your best bet for uncovering your talents is to explore your deep interests. Then, cultivate those strengths that are recognized in the marketplace. After thirty years of research, Harvard business psychologists Timothy Butler and James Waldroop conclude, "There are eight core business functions— not functions like marketing, sales, and finance—but basic activities such as quantitative analysis, theory development, perceptual thinking, managing people, enterprise control, and creative production. If you look at your deep interests and think about how those can be expressed in specific business behaviors, then you'll have the elements of a good career decision" (Butler and Waldroop offer a sample career self-assessment test on-line: www.careerdiscovery.com).

This is wise advice, but it doesn't necessarily apply to a small segment of the population. Even thinking of business activities in the broadest sense, you may not comfortably fit into Butler and Waldroop's business/work model. Your beloved thing may be playing a sport or performing modern dance, neither of which readily translates into commercial viability. It's an awfully competitive marketplace out there, with some mighty talented people scraping to make a living at their various passions. Unless our culture takes a U-turn, only a handful of souls can make a living writing poetry, playing chess, or making sculpture.

Do What You Love, the Money Will Follow is a lovely notion and an ideal to shoot for, but you can't count on it. It's often necessary to sacrifice our purse to our passions—and vice versa. Of course, this is an old story; the reason it needs mentioning again is it hasn't fully sunk in or been faced squarely. Playwrights or dancers who can't "make it" tend to feel deficient and employment-challenged, as if they've flunked grownup school. The truth is, however, that our culture/economy supports about as many full-time poets or puppeteers as National League shortstops. Making a living at such passions should be considered a gift; it's more realistic to regard these inspirations as one might a child—something to be nurtured, tended to, and sacrificed for. Thinking more along those lines can free you up to consider your economic life as part of the multidimensional puzzle of living fully.

By directly addressing your work dilemma, you can come up with the most palatable plan-B strategy—instead of just falling into something. Work done to support your love can still be satisfying. Assuming you like talking about your passion as well as doing it, there's always teaching, of course. If that doesn't work for you, consider finding a job that uses your second- or third-string interests. Or look for something that addresses different parts of you. A novelist working alone all day may welcome bartending or waitressing a couple nights a week. As noted earlier, there's always mercenary part-time or short-term jobs that pay well—including those that could allow you to build savings to supplement your income over a lifetime.

And don't forget that a modest spending life gives you

more work freedom—a small price to pay for pursuing your muse. As Lewis Hyde put it in *The Gift*, "The artist can tolerate a certain plainness in his outer life. I do not mean cold or hunger, but certainly the size of the room and the quality of the wine seem less important to a man who can convey imaginary color to a canvas. When the song of one's self is coming all of a piece, page after page, an attic room and chamber pot do not insult the soul."

EXERCISES FOR EXPLORING YOUR TALENTS

- Try keeping a work diary and note when things seem to go easily for you—and what you get compliments on.
- Write down the strengths you think you have in one column and in the other column verification for why that's so. After noting about ten in whatever order they come to mind, prioritize them according to what you're best at.
- What do you consider to be your greatest accomplishment?
- Psychologist Howard Gardner established the theory that humans have eight different kinds of intelligence. His ideas have gained wide acceptance among educators and psychologists who've seen that standard IQ tests are inadequate for assessing the full range of human intelligence.

  Everyone has some aptitude for each kind of intelligence, but in different proportions. The idea isn't to categorize yourself or anybody else as a certain type but to see which form of mental representation you favor or are most facile with. This can help you find where your greatest talents lie.

Look at the following types of intelligence and think about which you're best at:

Logical-mathematical: Good at and enjoy analyzing, problem solving, and strategy.

Spatial: Includes the artistically inclined as well as those who like rearranging objects/fiddling with machines.

Musical: You've got rhythm and beat.

Linguistic: Refers to the gift of playing with words and stories.

Interpersonal: Refers to social skills. How are you at relating to people? Those with strong interpersonal skills are often natural leaders.

Bodily-kinesthetic: Cut from the Wayne Gretzky or MJ cloth.

Intrapersonal: Refers your ability to understand and sense your "self." Intrapersonal intelligence allows us to understand who we are and what we're feeling. Obviously good for counselor/therapist sorts.

Naturalist: Yes, get outdoors or work to protect it.

- Ask a friend who knows you well and whose judgment you trust to list your top five strengths and give reasons why.
- For an even fuller, more objective self-view, in a compassionate but honest spirit, have a group of intimate friends talk about each other's strengths and weaknesses. If it's too hard to be honest face-to-face, have everyone write down four or five positives and negatives and print them out from a computer (which makes it impossible to distinguish who wrote what). How well does what others say correspond with how you see yourself?

WHY VALUES REALLY MATTER

Generational egotism may lead us to regard right livelihood as an invention of the sixties, but almost 2,400 years before Woodstock and the Kent State protests, Aristotle noted, "Where the needs of the world and your talents cross, there lies your vocation." A century before that, the Buddha actually coined the term *right livelihood*, making it a cornerstone of the Eightfold Path—his prescription for spiritual well-being. The Buddha believed we take on and embody traits from our job. Sell shoddy cars all day and you'll become shoddy, even after leaving the showroom.

Combine the advice of these (arguably the wisest men in history) and we see how important it is to do work that engages our talents and our soul. Values matter—a lot.

Incorporating values into your work isn't *just* about being a nice guy or racking up points for the afterlife. Practically speaking, the best reason to take your values seriously is, it enhances your work life. Values give you a sense of purpose and meaning. These, in turn, give you the commitment and energy to stick with challenging work. Taking values seriously can even pay off monetarily, since you're likely to develop a reputation for honest, quality work. Call it enlightened self-interest.

Inspired by the big, awakened guy himself, E. F. Schumacher gave a fuller definition of right livelihood in *Good Work*:

- To provide necessary and useful goods and services.
- To enable us to use and thereby perfect our gifts and talents like good stewards.
- To engage in this work in service to and in cooperation

with others, which helps liberate us from our inborn egocentricity.

But more important, what does right livelihood mean to you? What values and issues are most meaningful for you? What do you feel is worth fighting for?

After giving thought to your core values, you have to figure out how to manifest them for pay. Ideally, your work satisfies your interests, talents, and values directly, but often they won't neatly overlap. Most commercial endeavors are, at best, morally neutral. Yet there's usually a way to combine what you like to do and doing good—if somewhat tangentially. With so much room for improvement in this world of ours, there's an infinite number of ways to help. So if landscaping is your thing, don't feel like a louse because you don't work for the Red Cross. You can use your landscaping know-how to transform a ramshackle corner, inspire inner-city residents, be a truly equal opportunity employer, offer sliding-scale fees, show kids they can change their surroundings, and be environmentally sensitive. It's unlikely you'll do all of these at once, but the point is, you should be able to be true to yourself and, in some way, do your part to make the world a better place.

EXERCISES

- Forget realism for a moment. Imagine your utopian vision of the world and the country, as well as your community and your life. Later focus on the most essential aspects of each and see if you can imagine a way to help actualize them.

- Come up with a list of principles that you'd never want to compromise in a work situation. Then keep the list handy. This will make it easier to stick to them when faced with a dilemma.
- What injustice gets you most angry?
- What quality do you most admire in others?
- Are you leading a multiple life? If so, what are the benefits and costs of living this way? Can you find overlap between your career and other parts of yourself? If so, what does this suggest about cultivating greater integrity and impact in your work?
- What was your most principled stand—and what did you stand up for?
- Write down ten things you deeply value. Then prioritize them until you have your top five.
- Whom do you most want to serve? How many do you want to reach? Finish the sentence "For me, making a contribution means . . ."

PUTTING IT ALL TOGETHER

Each of us is the author of our own life story. How we interpret and narrate our own past and envision our future largely determines our fate. The quality of our imagination, our sense of adventure, and the questions we ask affect the plot and tone of our existence.

Novelists often structure a story around an idea or a powerful central question—often uncertain *exactly* where that inquiry will lead (typically, the writer only discovers "answers" herself as the characters develop and the plot unfolds). To keep our own story interesting, we can do the same thing; by focusing our life on issues that really matter and asking quality questions—even if they are unanswerable—we'll get a quality life.

After doing the self-inquiry in the previous sections you probably have several different themes that interest you. Now it's time to weave them together as best you can around one central issue. You can't expect to get everything just right; naturally there will be revisions along the way, and most probably the finished product will look considerably different from the first draft. But the idea is to have something you can work with. Remember, the first draft is always the hardest, but there's no other way to start.

CREATING A PERSONAL MISSION STATEMENT

Just as a business should be able to express its raison d'être on the back of a business card, you should be able to do that for your work life. Bringing such focus to your purpose both hones what you're really after and helps turn it into a reality. A personal mission statement is the condensed blueprint of your financial engine—your earning power. When that's working well, the rest of your finances are likely to flow smoothly.

Anyone who's gotten even a whiff of business-management philosophy knows that mission statements are a big deal. There are whole seminars, books, and retreats devoted solely to creating, revising, and testing mission statements. While some of this fervor may be overkill, there is good reason for the fuss. A mission statement is an organization's guiding light, its DNA. A good mission statement points the whole company, from mail clerk to CEO, in the same direction. *Personal* mission statements serve a similar function; they can keep us moving forward without getting sidetracked by tendencies to noodle, fantasize, and avoid the hard stuff.

A good mission statement should coalesce all you've learned about your talents, loves, personality, and values. It should consider the context of your whole life, including relationships and your long-term aspirations. It should speak to you in an intimate way, ideally centered more on process than ends. Notice the difference between deciding you want to be the best writer you can be and resolving to have three novels published within the next five years. The first gives direction and purpose without creating pressure. The second promotes rigidity and stress.

Creating goals that allow breathing room is an art. Remembering that they are truly for you (and free from others' expectations) can help you produce a guiding principle, not a taskmaster. Psychologists tell us good goals actually reduce stress; having guidelines gives a feeling of greater control and makes choices easier to handle.

Think of your mission statement as your personal constitution (open to amendments, of course). If it's thoughtfully constructed, it offers a compass when things get overwhelming. It's a reminder of what you want most, helping you prioritize and keep the bigger picture—*your* bigger picture—in mind. This, in turn, makes it easier to insist on quality work, be patient, and live a balanced life.

Write your mission statement down. This shows your commitment and grants it respect; otherwise, it can easily remain a wish or a hope. Although the point isn't accomplishments per se, it's nice to know that studies indicate writing goals down makes them more likely to happen. Focusing gives you power: a laser beam uses the same amount of energy as an ordinary lightbulb, but because all of its energy is concentrated, it can cut through steel.

Here's how to do it: Answer the questions "What am I here for? What gives my life meaning?" The part that guides your working life should include whom you want to serve and how, the scope of the impact you hope to make, and what skills you want to develop. Write as much as you like, but try to edit it back to a paragraph. Remember, its purpose is to help you focus. This exercise helps you think coherently about your priorities—making sense of the pieces of your collage. The process of creating a declaration of purpose is as important as the product.

REALITY TESTING

Visioning exercises and mission statements tend to make a spirit soar; putting a plan into action can turn a gut queasy. Like it or not, we live in a competitive world. This doesn't mean only brutes prosper, but it does demand savvy and skills to get what you want.

Even after insightful self-assessment exercises and creating an elegant mission statement, you'll probably still have decisions to make. Recognizing that feminist publishing is your passion, for example, still leaves many details to figure out. Do you want to publish confidence-boosting books for girls, put out a nonprofit newsletter for women in crisis, land a job as an editor, or write poetry?

Refining your preference will require research. Start with your first choice and learn all you can. Go to the library, interview those practicing your desired "craft," and get whatever real, hands-on experience you can. After completing your legwork, assess your skills. Then you can make a realistic plan, which may include an apprenticeship or schooling phase.

There is a Japanese martial arts proverb that goes "Zen seven, ken three." Zen refers to one's inner approach; the ken part, to one's technical ability or mastery of skill. In other words, having heart, discipline, inner strength, and resourcefulness are most important, but without know-how your endeavor won't fly.

Research requires patience. It may even be tedious, but doing it right can save untold heartache later. This is especially true if you're starting your own business. "Little" mistakes can be very expensive. For this reason, if you're starting a new enterprise in an industry you're unfamiliar with, start small. You can always build as you gain competence.

When you've done the whole shebang—soul-searching, mission statement, and research—and you still can't settle on one thing or you want confirmation before making a big commitment, consider holding a Quaker-style "clearness" meeting on your own behalf. It's like seeking help from your own board of directors.

Ask two to five people you trust (ideally with a facilitator) to entertain and discuss your thoughts, values, feelings, and dilemmas regarding the path(s) you're considering. You're looking more for clarity than for them to supply answers. Your "board" should mirror back what they are hearing, examine your assumptions, and offer alternatives. If your "directors" are up for it, follow-up meetings can be helpful. When gathering a small "board" together at once isn't feasible, speak to each member individually, but with the same idea of seeking clarity.

WHAT CAN GET IN OUR WAY AND WHAT WE CAN DO ABOUT IT

Assuming we don't have to take a dismal job, it's typically self-sabotage or an inability to shake dollar-fever that keeps us from satisfying work—both often the result of subconscious beliefs. Changing those thought patterns is no small task, so treat yourself compassionately. Create a healthy environment for yourself: cut back on exposure to commercialism and competitive workplaces, surround yourself with friends heading in the same direction, and read books you find inspiring.

We all know creative, intelligent, and dynamic people who never find satisfying work. Usually the problem is fear—fear of pain and sacrifice, fear of commitment, and/or fear of failure (often the result of high expectations). While there is no formula for clearing away dread, it can help to at least view the fear as a roadblock instead of the end of the road. What follow are a few timeless reminders that can take a lifetime to master.

First, try holding your efforts lightly. Working toward a goal without taking yourself too seriously is an art. The secret seems to lie in valuing process and best effort over results. A "being" (as opposed to "getting") orientation gives immediate feedback as to how you're doing. It also makes it easier to relax and work intuitively (thus, ironically, improving performance).

Second, don't compare yourself with anyone else. For one thing, we rarely even do it fairly. We tend to envy or measure ourselves against only one aspect of another person instead of taking the whole person in context. We may, for example, be jealous of our neighbor's tax bracket while ignoring the long hours he puts in at the job, the strain that creates on his family, and the insecurity that fuels his drive. We can learn plenty from others, but remember that comparing ourself with them is a losing game.

Third, accept—and work with—the limits that accompany a narrowing of career choices. Many of us resist limits of any kind, but to focus our energies, we must not only accept constraints but impose them on ourselves. As a family friend (who could never settle on anything himself) said, you can do anything you want, but not everything. Every truly creative endeavor—whether it's painting, poetry, or music—

requires dedication and operates within limits of form. Even Bo Jackson couldn't be his best when he played both football and baseball.

Last, recognize that positive change takes time. The desire for dramatic self-improvement is more likely to be a hindrance than a help since it makes us less likely to pay attention to process.

THE ALMOST-LAST THOUGHT

The idea of doing all these steps—soup to nuts—can make a body tired. It's tempting to just wing it, figuring that everything will work out. That may be true, but more likely it will work about as well as a novel written without any forethought to its basic structure. When you consider you're essentially planning for the rest of your life, investing the time to do your career search right makes sense. If you wing it wrong, you've not only spent lots of energy climbing up the wrong tree, you must disentangle yourself before starting again.

EXERCISES

- Create a mission statement.
- List three appropriate careers that fulfill your work mission. Do enough research so you can vividly imagine what your day and personal environment would be like in each.
- After you have a good understanding of what each

career entails, compare that reality to your mission statement and what you've learned about yourself. Are they a good fit?

- Write down the skills and knowledge required for the work you're considering. Grade yourself on how you match up on each of these. Then figure out how you'd make up for any shortfalls (with schooling, job experience, seminars, and so forth) and how long it would take.

- After deciding what you want to do, write yourself a note explaining why. If your decision doesn't work out well, at least you can see what, if anything, was wrong with your reasoning—and how it can be improved next time.

- Do litmus tests to see if you've found the right work. Do you:

Look forward to going to work?
Feel energized (most of the time) by what you do?
Feel that your contribution is respected, appreciated, and important?
Feel proud when describing your work to others?
Enjoy and respect the people you work with?
Feel optimistic about your future?

PART 5

GIVING IT AWAY

ADDING SOME SAVVY TO YOUR GENEROSITY

*It is more difficult to give money away intelligently
than earn it in the first place.*
—ANDREW CARNEGIE

Giving money away seems as if it should be easy. After all, the hard part is making it. Yet the charitable side of the equation can be tricky, too. First, there's getting over the impulse to keep it all for yourself; then there are questions of just how much to give away—and to whom? How do you assess who's worthy of your hard-earned gelt? And how can you maximize the impact of those gifts? Learning a bit about the tax code isn't exactly enticing, but it can allow us to give more.

Then there are the sometimes tricky issues associated with financial life after death. Sophisticated estate planning is among the most complex areas of personal finance. But for most people—even most moderately wealthy people—the strategies discussed here are quite accessible. And once you're hip to the rewards of a little planning, you'll wonder why no one told you about this stuff before.

After-life financial planning is probably the most neglected

of all personal finance topics. Yet it is one of the most important to heed. Ironically, many people who spend a lifetime
shopping for CD rates, loading up on tax-free municipal
bonds, and sheltering income in IRAs ignore dealing with their
exiting plans—not realizing that Uncle Sam can scalp more
than half of their life savings when they die (and in the case of
retirement plans, sometimes taking as much as 75 percent).

Baby boomers stand to inherit the largest transfer of financial assets in human history—more than $10 trillion. Unless
some thought and action are taken to steer those funds to
family or nonprofits we're passionate about, a good chunk of
it will go to Congress's latest brainchild.

HOW MUCH SHOULD WE GIVE?
(GENEROSITY WITHOUT TEARS—OR GUILT)

Despite our fondest hopes otherwise, morals and knowledge can be uncomfortably demanding. Knowing that countless starve while we sip a double latte or worry about traveling funds for our retirement leaves us with the nagging sense that we could be doing more. How much more is the tough question. Philosophers much wiser than I can argue both sides of the dilemma well: For the strict utilitarian, buying yourself anything more than regular meals and modest shelter is morally indefensible when others are suffering. For the individualist, pursuing reasonable joys—such as buying a good stereo and Pavarotti CDs—is so fundamental to the human soul that giving up everything, even in the name of helping mankind, is too much to expect (or some would say, want).

Unless we come down squarely on one side of these arguments, and can actually abide by it without regret, we must live with some paradox. Like riding two horses at once, handling this dilemma requires a combination of spurs and sugar—pushing ourselves to increase what we give while knowing we aren't creating financial hardship for ourselves.

Not surprisingly, few need worry about pushing their financial limits in the name of philanthropy. In 1995 the average American spent $161 a year more on dry cleaning than charitable donations. And those who give away a lot don't seem to suffer for it. In *They Gave Away a Fortune*, interviews with philanthropists who've given away all, or large chunks, of their wealth found that not one experienced any regret, even years later.

For most of us, the $64-billion question is how to expand what we give—and how to do it in a way that feels organic and rewarding. That middle ground won't satisfy those with a Mother Teresa spirit, but it can legitimately ease nagging guilt for the rest of us.

As with any financial reckoning, our charitable donations should reflect our bigger monetary picture. A couple with grown children and suitable retirement accounts earning $35,000 a year can afford considerably more charity than another couple with the same income, little savings, and three small kids. Neither is rich by U.S. standards, but there is room for lots more surplus for the older twosome.

Surveys show, however, that the *percentage* of giving doesn't increase with income or net worth. On average, multimillionaires donate about the same percentagewise as those earning $20,000 to $30,000 a year. Even taking lavish lifestyles into account, the living expenses for a millionaire tend to be considerably less percentagewise than for someone earning $50,000. That means they have lots more room to donate, not just dollarwise, but proportionally, without putting a crimp in their spending habits.

Charity can easily expand exponentially along with wealth. Rich folks can give away a lot and hardly affect their net worth, let alone their lifestyle. Tithing, while admirable and well intentioned, isn't the best way to approach donations—

much the way a progressive tax is fairer than a flat tax in a system that offers advantages for those on top.

Most Americans with assets could greatly expand their charitable donations—collectively adding $100 billion a year to good causes—with negligible effect on pleasurable spending and still have their net worth grow comfortably each year *after* adjusting for inflation.

Even lower-stratosphere, reasonably well-off sorts should consider their investments in the giving equation. Here's a simple method (adapted from Claude Rosenberg's *Wealthy and Wise*) for evaluating your ability to *comfortably* give:

1. Determine your surplus income and earning assets. *Surplus income* is what's left over after normal expenses, including taxes. *Earning assets* are those holdings that produce earnings. In other words, tally your stocks, bonds, money market, and any income-producing real estate. Don't include your house or vintage electric guitar.

2. Assuming you itemize on your tax returns, consider your donations on an after-tax basis. So if you're in the 30 percent tax bracket and gave $1,000 to charity, only $700 affects your financial condition.

3. Take that $700 and divide it into two parts. Compare each $350 to your surplus income and earning assets. So if you earned $10,000 more than you "needed" (that is, you were able to save $10,000) a year, you'd be giving away 3.5 percent of surplus income. If you had $200,000 in earning assets, you'd be giving away .175 percent—a mere pittance.

4. Naturally no one can tell you what percentage of your surplus to give away. But assuming inflation stays at its historical 3 percent and you earn an average 6.3 percent on

investments after tax (again, figuring the 30 percent tax bracket), you could give away 1 percent, or $2,000, of earning assets/investments and still have your investments grow faster than inflation.

For figuring donations based on your surplus income, compare your inflation-adjusted income growth to what your spending base was. For example, if you spent $40,000 and saved $10,000, you're still $8,800 ahead of inflation (which had decreased the buying power of your $10,000 savings by $1,200). That leaves plenty of room to donate more than the $350 and still significantly improve your financial condition.

No matter how you slice it, giving away more than $1,000 would hardly jeopardize your finances. It certainly allows you to give way more than the average $632, or 1.1 percent of *income*, that the typical $50,000 to $60,000 earner donates.

When you have a sizable investment portfolio, it's a good idea to make a five- or even ten-year charitable-giving plan, based on a projection of an 8 to 12 percent return on assets. That way, down markets won't dry up your giving for that year.

While the preceding method offers a safe and generous way to give without threatening your financial security, it may be too cautious for the bighearted with scant savings or relatively modest incomes. The traditional answer, then, is to donate or tithe a percentage of your income to charity. Some tithers are even convinced that their own good fortune depends on how generously they give money away. According to tradition, tithers give away 10 percent of their income. If you can't swing that, obviously it's better to do a smaller percentage and stick to it than to say you're going to do 10 percent but blow it off. You can always increase your percentage over time.

Whatever percentage you decide on, figure donations into an overall budget. When you consider that the average global income is $800 per year, making some sacrifice in the name of charity seems the least we can do. Generosity is defined by how much we can give, not absolute numbers. Imagining we'll give more when we have real financial security usually just means we never do it. Consider the cherry pie analogy: when you're hungry, the first piece is very satisfying, but by your second (or at most third) slice, you hardly taste it anymore. Rather than polishing off the dessert yourself, share some of it. Others will appreciate it more than you would, and you'll feel better—less bloated and lighter on your feet.

When you can't afford to give anything approaching a percentage of your income, try to donate time. In fact, even if you give away bundles, there's no substitute for hands-on helping. Research shows that regular volunteering (when you have direct contact with those whom you're helping) produces a "helper's high" that creates health benefits similar to regular exercise. Consistent, hands-on altruism reduces stress and can alleviate such chronic conditions as hypertension, arthritis, depression, headaches, and back pain.

WHO DESERVES YOUR DONATIONS? AND HOW TO GIVE THEM MORE OOMPH

If your mailbox looks anything like mine, you're popular with the nonprofit set. A never-ending flow of fund-raising gambits—from surveys, tote-bag offers, and calendars to outright pleas—besiege and cajole your conscience six days a week. Of course, the intentions behind most of these requests are of the highest order. There is, after all, no shortage of remedial work to be done. And since the government has cut back funding charities at the same time it's dismantling its own safety nets, individual contributions—which make up 80 percent of the typical nonprofit's budget—are more crucial than ever.

Yet worthy as these causes are, who can keep up with the barrage and still pay her heating bill? Responding to a few appeals here and there—sending out $15 when you're feeling guilty and $25 after picking this week's winning pony—is certainly better than nothing, but it's not the most effective way to spend your charitable dollars. Such a method mostly ensures that you fund those groups that excel at direct marketing. You may even end up supporting charlatan or masquerading front groups, whose real purpose is actually the opposite of what their name and literature imply.

Smart giving, not surprisingly, requires forethought. It

means prioritizing your concerns. It means finding nonprofits that can leverage your donations into long-term effective remedies and investigating how your money is actually being spent. It also means taking advantage of tax laws that allow you to maximize your donations.

WHERE TO BEGIN

The place to start is with yourself. Think about your values. What do you consider to be the top two or three issues to address? Obviously there are plenty of problems to choose from. The 1995 edition of *The Encyclopedia of World Problems* lists 13,167 major issues (up from 2,560 in 1976—a record of per annum increases that rivals the roaring bull market over a similar period). Naturally, trying to remedy any of these difficulties is great, but who can say which one needs to be worked on first? Almost all efforts are needed and worthy. It's simply a matter of prioritizing and deciding what matters most to you.

It may be hard to concentrate your donations and involvement on one or even a few problems to the exclusion of others, but if you try to take everything on, you're likely to spread yourself too thin—getting distracted and, in the long run, making less of an impact. Greater focus brings greater influence.

After settling on your areas of interest, do some homework. Confirm that the problem is as dire as you believe. Think about whether it can effectively be tackled through donations or volunteer work and find out if there is already ample funding addressing the issue. Most problems could absorb unlimited expenditures, but given that you probably have a limited budget, it is necessary to be discerning. Consider, for example, that Boys Town's village residential program spent $22.2 million in 1996 providing homes for 714 wayward children, or $31,231 per child. It seems reasonable to look at other ways—or certainly other organizations—to address problems of child neglect and abuse.

After deciding on your issues, get the names of several charities that specifically address that problem. With over a million nonprofit groups, there are lots of similar-sounding names out there. Some smaller groups even deliberately take names that sound like well-established organizations, hoping to sail in the large ships' wake. Don't assume that a group is a perfect fit just because of its name. Read a bunch of mission statements to find a handful of groups that are worth investigating more closely.

Consider looking for organizations that address the fundamental causes of problems. Take a page from those folks who do systems analysis and look for "leverage points"—those places within any complex system (an economy, a culture, a city, as examples) where a small shift in one thing can produce big changes throughout. This is going one step beyond the aphorism "Give a man a fish and he eats for a day; teach a man to fish and he eats forever." One could, for instance, ask and address such questions as: Why hasn't everyone learned to fish? Who owns the lake? And how do we change the rules governing the lake's use?

There are, for instance, many ways one could combat racism in Mississippi. A "teach 'em to fish" advocate might make a donation to the United Negro College Fund. An organization working on a leverage point, however, might—as the nonprofit Southern Echo did—seek to redraw election districts that don't reflect their constituency. An eighteen-month grassroots campaign in the early nineties by Southern Echo did just that, and it led to a doubling of African-American representatives in the state legislature. The Black Caucus then succeeded in procuring the highest education budget in Mississippi history.

The Internet is a great place to start your search for effective organizations. Some of the info on the Net is slightly dated, and many smaller groups can fall through the cracks, but you'd be amazed at how many organizations are covered. The Internet Nonprofit Center (www.nonprofits.org), for example, has basic IRS data on 1.2 million nonprofits. The Philanthropic Research Institute's GuideStar Web site (www2. guidestar.org) has even more detailed profiles on 600,000 charities and nonprofits.

For those without access to cyberspace, *The National Directory of Nonprofit Organizations,* by the Taft Group in Detroit, is the largest print directory, with basic information on 245,000 nonprofits. Gale Research's *Encyclopedia of Associations* doesn't cover as many charitable organizations but is more likely to be in your library.

Another excellent source of information is foundations. Foundations are in the business of giving money away. The larger ones have a staff that devotes itself to analyzing worthy causes. By asking a foundation that covers your area of interest for names of worthy nonprofits, you'll be taking advantage of its embodied knowledge.

For those with substantial wealth to distribute, there are philanthropic consultants happily willing (for a fee) to manage and help with your donation efforts. Or you may want to consider putting together your own mini–board of advisers who can help you direct your funds to good causes.

CHECKING THEM OUT

Unlike business, sports, or even bridge, the $150-billion nonprofit "industry" doesn't get regular media coverage. There are the occasional horror stories about fake charities, lavish expense accounts, or embezzlement à la United Way that make the front pages, but your less dramatic, more frequent problems of a bloated bureaucracy or poorly focused management receive scant coverage. Those types of articles don't make for catchy headlines and can even backfire on the newspaper reporting them, making the paper look mean-spirited. Finding out which charities are most worthy of donations will require some effort on your part.

If you're considering contributing to one of the country's largest charities, much of the research has already been done for you. Watchdog groups such as the National Charities Information Bureau (19 Union Square West, New York, NY 10003; [212] 929-6300; www.give.org) and the Better Business Bureau's Philanthropic Advisory Service (4200 Wilson Blvd., Arlington, VA 22203; www.bbb.org) keep tabs on over three hundred charities and rate them based on program spending and administration. Each agency has extensive information on-line, or you can request reports for a modest charge.

What contributors usually want to know most is, what percentage of their donation went to programs and what percentage to fund-raising. As a general rule of thumb, spending more than 25 to 30 percent on fund-raising is too much. Many groups manage to spend 85 or 90-plus percent on programs.

Checking out smaller groups not covered by the watchdog agencies (which is about 99.95 percent of all organizations) requires more legwork. Ask for a group's IRS Form 990 and annual report. Sometimes this information can be found on the Internet, but usually the Web info is at least a few years out of date—unless it's directly from the group's own site. The Contact Center Network's Nonprofit Website Directory (www.idealist.org) links you to over nine thousand individual charities' Web sites.

The IRS Form 990 looks like a tax return and is easy to decipher. It reveals a lot about a group's finances. A 990 lists expenditures for programs, fund-raising, and administration and highlights major uses of capital. Every charity that takes in more than $25,000 (except church groups) must file a 990 annually. Attachments to the 990 disclose how much the five highest-paid staff members earn as well as board members' compensation, if any. It also reveals monies paid to significant outside contractors or consultants. Proportion is, of course, important. The head of the Sierra Club, for example, pulls in $80,000-plus a year—rather modest for an operating budget of roughly $40 million but a red flag if the group's take were under $1 million.

By law, nonprofits must mail the past three years of tax filings to anyone who requests them (technically, the groups can ask to be reimbursed for the cost of copying and postage). Most groups will send potential donors a copy for free, but be prepared to make more than one phone call. Don't be put off if the receptionist says, "What's a 990?" But do be upset—and wary of a group's efficiency—if a few requests to the *right* person don't produce the documents. If you're not ready to give up on a group too incompetent to get you the 990s itself or are working on an exposé for *The Village Voice*, you can get the forms directly from the IRS, although it's a bit of a hassle.

In addition to 990s, ask for the current and past two annual reports. By following an organization's recent history, you can get a good sense of how well it has performed and where it's heading. Check out the income statement in the annual report first. An income statement basically shows you the flow of money—where it came from and where it went.

When it comes to program spending, don't accept percentages and dollar amounts at face value. Every group does its accounting a bit differently. Some count fund-raising appeals as an educational program expense. Sometimes they legitimately are, but if the majority of those dollars are spent on bulk mail, you have to wonder just how educational those appeals are. Having an accurate sense of how each group handles fund-raising and program expenses will let you compare apples to apples.

The more an organization relies on volunteers, the lower its expenses will be. Professional fund-raisers typically take at least 40 percent of the haul—and sometimes as much as 85 percent. For every $3 box of Girl Scout cookies you buy, only 30 to 50 cents goes to the Girl Scout treasury.

Keep in mind that while numbers are revealing, they have their limits. Groups that are fighting less popular causes or have a low profile often have higher expense ratios than household names like the Red Cross. The biggest groups often receive substantial government aid, which makes their fund-raising ratios look good.

Two opposite indicators to note in annual reports are

deficits and operating reserves. Obviously, increasing debt isn't a good sign. Less obvious is a concern for too much surplus. Philanthropy watchdogs suggest that holding more than two or three years of operating reserves is keeping too much for a rainy day and not putting enough into programs. You can calculate this number by dividing total available net assets by total annual expenses.

Note any qualifications in the CPA's auditor's opinion letter. If something sounds odd, do a double or triple take. And if you can't get acceptable answers, pass on that group.

Beyond the numbers, one way to learn more about a group is by probing the board of directors. How often does it meet? Is it a volunteer or paid board? How well represented are minorities and women (assuming that's an appropriate question)? Large boards tend to be ineffective and removed from what's really happening, often added more for figurehead appeal than actual advising. When the United Way scandal broke in 1992, among its sixty-member board was then IBM chairman John Akers and management shrewdie Bill Gates.

When there's a small board, are all the members from the same company or, worse yet, the same family? Seeking out an ex–board member can be very revealing, as he or she is likely to be forthcoming about the organization's strengths and weaknesses. Ask about staff turnover: that can indicate how committed and fired up the organization is.

For smaller groups you can always serve on the board yourself. This will give you excellent insights into the group's effectiveness. Volunteering for any variety of yeoman duties and talking to volunteers can also clue you in to how well a charity is run.

It's important to respect an organization's vision and

know-how and not be paternalistic in your giving, but don't be bashful about asking tough questions. Nonprofits are generally run with the best of intentions, but they do often face difficult ethical choices and administrative dilemmas. You have a right to know that your donations are being well spent. For example, it's fine to ask how many bowls a soup kitchen serves each week. Knowing specifics about how a charity is fulfilling its mission not only keeps a group on its toes, it gives you the confidence to really open your wallet.

IMPROVING YOUR CHARITABLE DOLLARS' IMPACT

The exercise of investigating nonprofits—settling on one or, at most, a few groups to concentrate on—and then consciously including charitable contributions in your overall budget is likely to increase the amount and impact of your giving. You'll become more knowledgeable about a few issues and proactive in your giving instead of merely reacting to requests that get your attention. In subsequent years you'll find that it becomes easier to track the progress and effectiveness of your favorite organizations. You'll be more likely to adjust your giving upward as your finances improve and feel comfortable writing bigger checks. You'll see that nothing bad happens when you give generously. If anything, you'll feel better: good about yourself and less guilty about passing on the countless direct-marketing appeals.

Making many small gifts is less efficient than making a few large ones; the smaller your gift, the bigger the share that goes to fund-raising. If you feel uncomfortable always saying no to all but a few charities, budget a small slush fund for telemarketers and door-to-door canvassers. (It still makes sense to ask whether the callers are volunteers or pros—and how much of your pledge will go to the charity.)

When making large donations, you can leverage your funding either by making the gift contingent on the charity's finishing some specific project or by offering it as a challenge or matching grant. If the nonprofit raises the amount you request, then you kick in your generous share. If your gift is big enough, you could jump-start a specific project by underwriting it. Before despairing that you'd never have enough *dinero* to pull that off, consider pooling funds with likeminded friends, neighbors, or family. Put together a few $1,000 and $100 pledges and you have a $5,000 endowment to offer. Do remember, however, that since change takes time, a one-time grant isn't as effective as making a multiyear commitment.

MAKING UNCLE SAM
YOUR CHARITABLE PARTNER

It may be distasteful to include the head of your accountant in matters of the heart, but combining the two allows your charitable dollars to go further. With a little know-how and a few smidgens of tax law awareness, charitable gifts will cost less—which allows you to give more.

DEDUCTING CASH CONTRIBUTIONS

Money given to charities can be written off on your taxes. So, within certain limitations, the more you give to non-profits, the less you pay to the IRS. Those limitations are noted below.

- By cash I don't mean the literal green stuff, of course. Outside of the few bucks you toss into the Salvation Army bucket, don't give actual greenbacks. Cash can't be documented as a contribution—and it leaves you susceptible to swindlers. If anyone claiming to represent a charity asks explicitly for cash, assume you're dealing with a horse thief (or worse).

While charitable fraud is small, sharks do exist, preying on kind-blooded and naïve souls. Consumer advocates recommend never divulging your credit card number over the phone no matter how nice the telemarketer sounds. If you have any questions about the legitimacy of a nonprofit after reading its annual report and IRS Form 990, ask your state attorney general's office if it has had any complaints.

- No, that "loan" you made to Uncle Jack to help him settle his gambling debts can't be deducted—even if it was with the altruistic intention of keeping Big Arnie's boys off his leg. A donation to Gamblers Anonymous, however, would count. Come tax time, the IRS only recognizes gifts to 501(c) (3)-registered organizations.

  Donations to lobbying groups, such as Handgun Control, are not tax-deductible. Often organizations like the Sierra Club, which do political lobbying, also have educational programs that maintain a tax-exempt status. You can still get write-offs by earmarking your checks to the educational programs.

- Any single donation of $250 or more requires a receipt from the charity, given at the time of the gift. Simply saving your canceled check for these larger deductions isn't enough for the IRS—and retroactive receipts won't fly in an audit.

- Cash gifts made to a public charity (generally charitable organizations that receive support from a variety of sources) can be written off up to 50 percent of the donor's adjusted gross income (AGI). Any amount over the 50 percent limit can be carried forward and deducted over the course of the next five years.

- Deductions of cash gifts to private foundations (typically, nonprofits funded by one person, family, or business) are limited to 30 percent of AGI, with the same five-year time limit for writing the full amount off.
- In November and December take a second look at your level of giving for the year. When you itemize your deductions on Schedule A—and even more important, if you itemize *every other year* (see page 72)—write your charitable checks before New Year's Eve if you want the deductions to count for that year's taxes.
- If you don't regularly itemize, consider putting your yearly charitable donations in an earmarked account, letting it build for a few years, and then giving it all at once. Let's say you normally give $1,000 a year. If you collected three years' worth of donations-to-be plus investment earnings and then gave it all at once, the $3,000-plus donation would probably be enough to put you over the standard deduction. Any investment tax savings could be added to your gift.

  The other way to, in effect, "bunch" charitable deductions is through a gift fund (see "Setting Up a 'Poor Man's Foundation'" later in the chapter).
- Don't rely on charities themselves for tax advice, particularly small ones that don't have departments specializing in such matters. Most organizations are stretched so thin, they can't hire a tax expert to keep up with the latest rule changes. If you act on their misguided advice, you'll pay the penalty, not them. When in doubt, check with an accountant or the IRS itself.

DONATING APPRECIATED ASSETS

The IRS rules governing deductions taken for assets that have appreciated in value are different from those which cover gifts of cash. Getting a sense of what these are can be used to your advantage, as well as your charity's—stretching the impact of your generosity.

- Stocks, bonds, mutual funds, and real estate that have appreciated in value make great charitable gifts because you get to write off their current market value and side-step capital gains taxes. So if you have $5,000 worth of Intel stock that cost you $1,000, you could give the shares to the charity of your choice and take the full $5,000 deduction—without paying the taxes due on the $4,000 profit.

  There are two caveats to remember, however: First, the asset must be considered a long-term gain—that is, you must have held it for at least eighteen months. Second, give the shares to the charity and have it sell them. Otherwise, the gain—and IRS levy—will still be in your name.

- Deductions of gifts of appreciated property are limited to 30 percent of your adjusted gross income for public charities and 20 percent for private foundations. As with cash gifts (which have yearly limits of 50 percent and 30 percent, respectively), any excess write-offs can be carried forward for five years.

- If you can't afford to give away fully appreciated property but want part of it to benefit a charity, sell the charity the asset at a below-market price—in effect, a bargain sale. You pay tax on any gain and get a deduction for the difference between what you sold the property for and what it's really worth. So if you sold your $5,000 Intel stock—which cost you $1,000—to the Environmental Defense Fund for $4,000, you'd owe taxes on a $3,000 gain and get a $1,000 write-off.

DEDUCTING AND DONATING OTHER STUFF

Donations to charities that involve noncash (or not readily convertible into cash) transactions have different rules to abide by. To stay on Uncle Sam's good side, heed the baker's half-dozen guidelines below.

- When you give something other than cash, it's your job to estimate its value; the charity is only responsible for providing a description of the items.
- For property worth more than $5,000 (other than readily marketable securities), you must have an independent appraiser value the item. Your mom's opinion ("Miró really outdid himself that time"), while valuable, won't cut mustard with the IRS. If it's a significant sum, you should have two appraisals done and use the average. The appraisal fees can be itemized on your Schedule A.
- Your volunteer time, although incredibly important to charitable efforts, isn't recognized by the IRS. Your wheels, however, are. Keep track of mileage you log doing charitable work, and if you itemize, you can write off 12 cents a mile. Miscellaneous unreimbursed expenses you incur when volunteering are also deductible.

- Any product and/or service you buy from a charity is only deductible for the amount *above* its "fair market value." So even if you hate Paul Anka and just bought the $150 front-row seats to support the benefit, you can still deduct only $110 (assuming the seats are worth $40). Likewise, that $1,500 Dalí print you bought at the hospital auction isn't deductible at all if it's actually worth $1,500.

- When donating art, antiques, rare books, or collectibles, note that you can only write off the full appraised amount of the objects if the charity uses them for a *"related purpose."* So if the artwork is to be exhibited or the antique chairs sat on, they can be deducted. But if the charity sells the painting or chairs immediately after receiving them, you can only deduct your cost—not their appreciated value.

- If you happen to be an artist or a craftsperson, the IRS doesn't hold a high opinion of your work, even if you're hot in Soho galleries. The only deductible part of a donated work you create yourself is the cost of materials.

- Donating the use of your vacation home for a fundraising auction is a generous way to help, but that value doesn't count as a charitable contribution. Worse yet, the bidder's use of your home could jeopardize your deduction for rental expenses, as his vacation time counts toward the fourteen-day or 10 percent personal usage limit that disallows the property from being considered a rental unit (which comes with tax benefits).

SETTING UP A "POOR MAN'S FOUNDATION"

You no longer have to be rich to establish the equivalent of your own foundation. In fact, for generous souls who have a modest lifestyle and some savings, *gift funds* are a shrewd way to make donations.

Traditionally, wealthy philanthropists established foundations for tax write-offs and the legacy of having their name live on connected with largesse. The income and appreciation from their foundation's investments could theoretically fund charitable disbursements in perpetuity (or until that big asteroid hits). The problem with starting a private foundation is, foundations require *at least* $250,000 to create, cost from $2,000 to $5,000 to start up, and incur ongoing administrative and investment management fees, including a 2 percent annual excise tax. Cash gifts to private foundations (as noted earlier in the chapter) are deductible only up to 30 percent of adjusted gross income.

With a charitable gift fund, you can essentially create the same institution with as little as $10,000 (subsequent contributions must be $2,500 or more)—and get better benefits. Since gift funds are considered public charities, you get advantages private foundations don't: you can write off more of your donations against your income; you don't have to give away a minimum of 5 percent every year; you don't have to keep books and file foundation tax returns; you pay no setup charges; and you pay only a 1 percent (as opposed to 2 percent) administrative fee. It won't even cost your ego much: even though you aren't setting up your own freestanding institution, you can name your gift fund account whatever you'd like; your charitable recipients will know who their benefactor is.

For the "simple liver" who has some savings, but not enough expenses (such as mortgage interest, gambling losses, and real estate taxes) to justify itemizing on Schedule A, a charitable gift fund can work great. One sizable gift will allow you to write off expenses and contributions beyond the standard deduction, yet you don't have to give away all the money that year. Make your donations whenever you please. The only restriction is, they must be for $250 or greater.

When you use appreciated assets for gifts, the tax savings are even better. In addition to write-offs, you also get to bypass the capital gains tax you would have owed (see "Donating Appreciated Assets" on page 249 for details). A gift fund donation may be especially appealing if you have one large, jackpot investment.

Let's say, for instance, that your $200 stake in BioTech Associates, purchased years ago on a tip from your chiropractor, turns into $200,000 after the company discovers *the* cure for cancer. You're willing to give away $100,000 of that "found" money but don't want to donate it all at once (or attract hordes of fund-raisers to your door, since they'll assume you're loaded).

Putting the hundred grand in a gift fund eliminates the tax liability on $99,800 of the profit, gives $100,00 in write-offs, and lets you take your time deciding what good use you'll put it to. If you gave away $7,000 a year and invested the balance in the stock market, there's a good chance you could make large donations for the rest of your life and the principal would keep growing.

Gift funds also work nicely for anyone who is ready to make a big gift but isn't sure exactly whom she wants to give it to yet. You can be generous when the spirit moves you and then concern yourself with the details later.

How do you set up one of these gift funds? At this writing there are only two places to go, although more promise to be on the way soon. The most established game in town is Fidelity Investment's Charitable Gift Fund ([800] 682-4438), which pioneered the genre. PNC Bank ([888] 844-1565) has a fund that is available in ten states. Merrill Lynch and Vanguard are exploring the possibility and may well have something by the time this book goes to press.

FINANCIAL LIFE AFTER DEATH

O f course, we both know we're too young to die, but let's face it: even if we eat organic kale twice a week and fast on the solstice, it's gonna happen at some point—and we never know when. I'm not suggesting you set up a trust if you're a robust twenty-five-year-old with little to your name except an outstanding student loan, but after-life financial planning isn't just for those who believe in reincarnation. Even if you can't take it with you, your money lives on—either helping people or causes you care about, causing squabbles among those left behind, or filling government coffers. Here are a few reasons to pay attention to estate-planning issues, even if the topic initially strikes you as about as enticing as a Saturday night insurance seminar:

- A will is a must for every adult—especially if you've got kids. If you die without making your wishes known, lots can go wrong with both your children's guardianship and your assets. Dying without a will is at best inconsiderate and at worst tragic to the survivors. Amazingly, over 80 percent of parents with young children have no formal instructions specifying who should care for their little ones in the event of their death.

- If you have an "alternative lifestyle"—that is, if you are *not* married to your significant other, whether gay or straight—estate planning requires even closer attention. Without a will or other arrangements, the law won't recognize your partner's claim to any of your things, even if you want him or her to have everything.
- Any couple with over $650,000[1] in assets, which includes payouts from insurance policies, could be subject to estate taxes. They should explore ways to minimize or eliminate those taxes, including options for charitable giving.
- Regardless of your marital status, wealth, or health, anyone who has reached the half-century mark with any sort of assets should familiarize herself with estate-planning issues. This will help you plan for the future with a sense of what's up ahead.
- Even if none of the preceding situations directly applies to you, there's a good chance estate planning is something your parents should pay attention to. I'm not recommending that you hound them ("Hey, Dad, have you put me in your will yet?"), but since 70 percent of American adults don't even have a will, it's likely they need a little prodding on the matter.

It may sound unseemly to ask your parents to look into their exiting financial plans, but a little forethought can go a long way toward avoiding heavy estate taxes and probate fees while perhaps also reassuring them that you don't need all their savings.

By talking things over with your parents, you can en-

---

1. In 1999 $650,000 is the trigger point for estate taxes, but that figure will gradually rise until it is $1 million in 2006. Note that money passes tax-free between spouses, regardless of the amount.

courage them to enjoy their money themselves and/or recommend they donate some (or all) of their assets to charity. Planned giving, if done right, can give them current tax and financial benefits as well as great satisfaction. Knowing they're contributing to a worthy cause that reaches beyond their own life adds dignity to their death and gives some comfort from the pain of passing on. Many potential benefactors who could afford to be generous don't because they feel too guilty about denying their heirs money. If you're financially comfortable yourself, letting your parents know you're okay without their financial help can free them to pursue meaningful philanthropy. Talking openly and jointly about the whole family's financial state will make significant decisions that everyone feels at home with easier.

WHERE THERE'S A WILL, THERE'S A WAY TO SORT THINGS OUT

If you don't have a will, you should. Otherwise, when you die, two unpleasant things can happen. First, your heirs may disagree about who should get what. (This can happen even when there is a will that isn't specific enough about property designations.)

Second, without a will, all your possessions and assets will be given away according to state formula, not your wishes. This can lead to some unfortunate distributions. Your hostile, right-wing Uncle Ernie, for example, may get all your worldly possessions instead of your unmarried lover if Ernie turns out to be your only next of kin. Or in some states, without a will, it's likely that your young children would inherit half or even two-thirds of your estate, leaving your spouse with fewer assets or less control than you'd like. In other states your ninety-year-old mother could automatically get a third of your estate unless you had indicated otherwise. Of course, all those arrangements might be fine with you, but that's probably not how you would have done it if you had had your way.

You don't need a lawyer to create a valid will. Most wills are reasonably simple documents. Computer software and three witnesses can create a competent will for most basic estates.

If your assets are greater than $650,000 or if your life, financial or otherwise, is even slightly complicated,[2] check with a lawyer who has experience drawing wills. Attorney fees are typically modest for setting up a will (it's generally considered a loss leader for more expensive probate or estate-planning work). You can probably lower that bill even further by setting the will up yourself first with software or a preset form and then asking a lawyer to double-check the document. Ask her to be particularly attentive to laws that are unique to your state.

It's easy to donate money to nonprofit groups or foundations through your will. Simply state (or add, if you already have an established will)[3] in the document: "I give, devise, and bequeath to _____ [put name and address of charitable organization] the sum of $_____, to be

---

2. Complications would include (but not be limited to) having an heir who is mentally impaired, young, or a spendthrift; anticipating that someone may contest the will; having more than one set of children; wanting to establish a trust; or having a significant ownership stake in a private business.
3. A *codicil*, or addition, to a will requires witnesses.

used for its general purposes [or whatever particular program you're interested in supporting]." Instead of indicating an exact dollar amount to donate, consider putting it as a percentage of your assets. That way, should late-in-life medical costs greatly diminish your estate, a charity won't end up with $20,000 while your spouse gets $2,000. You also may want to make your gift contingent on your beneficiaries' predeceasing you.

As detailed later in the chapter, another good reason to include charities in your will is any monies willed to a tax-exempt charity reduce the value of your estate—a real consideration when your assets are over $650,000, since federal and possibly state taxes will take a big chunk anyhow.

If your estate will be in the serious seven- or eight-figure territory, reflect on the effect any inheritance will have on your beneficiaries. For some it will free them up to do creative and helpful work; for others it will be guilt-inducing and/or sap initiative. According to psychologist John Levy, who has worked with clients inheriting fortunes, those beneficiaries "who came from families where philanthropy is valued as a central part of life turn out to be much better off [emotionally and psychologically] than those who don't."

TWO MORE MAINSTAYS FOR THE PREPARED: A LIVING WILL AND DURABLE POWER OF ATTORNEY

A *living will* is not a part of your will. It is a separate document that states what kind of medical care you do—and more important, do not—want should you become terminally ill or permanently unconscious. It becomes effective only when you're not. A living will is, in essence, a contract with your attending doctor to honor your conscious requests—typically, a refusal of life support if there is no chance for recovery. Living wills make difficult decisions easier for your family. They are also a significant part of estate planning because intensive medical costs are astronomical, easily eating up a lifetime of savings.

A *durable power of attorney* can take two forms: one is for health care and the other for financial matters. A durable power of attorney for health care or a *health-care proxy* is similar to a living will except you are entrusting someone you know to make sure doctors are following your wishes.

A financial power of attorney (which some states require to be a separate document from a health-care one) appoints a trusted person to handle your financial affairs should you become incapacitated. Like the health-care designation, a financial power of attorney allows you to name an unmarried partner or friend to make crucial decisions for you. Without that designation, if your family were against it, under state law a non–family member wouldn't be allowed to participate in decisions about your financial affairs. Needless to say, before designating anyone to have power of attorney, discuss it with him.

ON DEATH AND TAXES:
AT LEAST ONE CAN BE AVOIDED

Federal estate taxes kick in at $650,000. The first dollars over $650,000 are taxed at 37 percent, and that rate climbs as high as 55 percent for property over $3 million. In addition to federal estate taxes, nineteen states impose *inheritance* taxes on beneficiaries. Typically, the inheritance tax rate depends on your relationship to the deceased. In Nebraska, for example, a friend would have to pay a 15 percent inheritance tax on $25,000 she received, while your child would pay only 1 percent. Except for Massachusetts, Mississippi, New York, and Ohio, all states have abolished estate (but not inheritance) taxes above and beyond the federal levy.

There are a variety of ways to dodge or minimize estate taxes. The simplest is to give money away. Anything donated to nonprofit groups above the $650,000 threshold is excused from your estate's value.

The IRS is deaf to gifts to individuals up to $10,000. Since the $10,000 tax-free gift exclusion is per person, a couple can effectively give away $20,000 to any individual. If your gift recipient is married, a couple could pass on $40,000 a year ($20,000 to you and $20,000 to your partner) without exciting the tax man. Directly paying someone else's medical bills or school tuition isn't subject to the $10,000 limit.

WHEN TO TRUST A TRUST

Trusts are legal entities created to own property and direct its distribution. They exist only on paper. You transfer assets to a trust to navigate postdeath financial waters—that is, to avoid probate, reduce estate taxes, and/or ensure that assets reach the appropriate hands. Trusts come in many flavors, offering a variety of options, depending on your goals and financial situation. The more common trusts aren't expensive or complicated to set up, even though they typically involve the services of an estate attorney.

Trusts are not just for the jet-setting rich. Gay partners with modest assets, for example, may want to set up a *living trust* for extra protection against challenges to their will. A couple with more than $650,000 may want to create a *bypass trust* to essentially double their estate tax protection. And anyone who wants to give money to charity while receiving tax deductions and retaining some of their investment's benefits while still alive may want to use one of the charitable trusts (or one of their derivative variations that can be funded with as little as $5,000).

The following are brief descriptions of the most common trusts and those used to benefit charities. It's not a comprehensive listing, as there are others, such as a grantor-retained trust, which are typically used for planning for multimillion-dollar estates and require the assistance of expert legal hands.

Bypass Trust. The bypass, or AB, trust (also known as a unified credit trust or credit shelter trust) is the most popular trust in estate planning. It is well suited for married couples with grown children who want to pass on up to $1.3 million of their assets tax-free—essentially doubling their estate tax exclusion. The way it works is, both spouses put their assets in the trust. When one of them dies, his half, or up to $650,000, goes to the children—with the crucial provision that the other spouse can use that money for the rest of her life. Technically, the surviving spouse is only entitled to the trust's income and 5 percent of the principal yearly (or $5,000, depending on whichever is more). But the trustee (the trust's supervisor) has the right to give the remaining partner any part of the principal needed for general support or to pay medical bills. Basically, this allows you to "give away" the cake and eat it, too.

Living Trust. The raison d'être for a living trust is to avoid *probate*, the often long and expensive process of having a court validate and administer a will. Without a living trust, any assets of a deceased person that do not have designated beneficiaries (that is, everything *but* retirement accounts, insurance policies, or joint-ownership accounts) undergo probate. Attorney fees typically eat up 5 to 7 percent of an estate during probate, and the will goes into public records.

Transferring your assets to a living trust avoids all that and sidesteps anyone who wants to contest your heirs' inheritance. Living trusts keep your property holdings a private matter. The beneficiaries of a living trust can be changed anytime you want, but upon your death, all your stuff passes directly to them. The potential downside of a living trust is, it doesn't shield your assets from estate taxes. So usually, if you have over $650,000 in assets, it's not the way to go.

Note that even if you set up a living trust, you should still have a will. That way, any assets or property you've forgotten to transfer to your living trust will still go to the person(s) you wish.

Life Insurance Trust. While proceeds from life insurance policies aren't subject to *income* tax or probate, they are considered part of an estate. Uncle Sam automatically becomes one of your beneficiaries if your insurance policy payout puts your estate over $650,000. To disinherit the ubiquitous uncle, you can put the insurance payout into a trust. Typically, your spouse gets income from the trust and can even use its principal if needed. After he or she dies, the remaining assets go to the beneficiaries named in your trust. Moving a life insurance policy to a life insurance trust is about the easiest way to transfer money estate tax–free.

There are a few caveats to note about a life insurance trust. First, should there be any cash value in your life insurance policy, you can't touch it once it's been moved to a trust. Second, if there is more than $10,000 in cash value in your policy, the trust's recipient will incur a gift tax (not so if there are multiple beneficiaries and none of them receives more than $10,000). Third, should you die within three years of establishing a life insurance trust, the payout is considered part of your estate. For that reason your attorney will include a provision that, in effect, cancels the trust should you die within that time limit.

Spendthrift Trust. Not all heirs are competent to handle their financial affairs. If one of your beneficiaries is too young, mentally impaired, or out of control, you can establish a trust that pays him incrementally.

CHARITABLE TRUSTS

Death and taxes may be inevitable, but charitable trusts can soften the blow of each. Bequeathing a gift to a charitable group can ensure that your ethics and efforts live on while also giving tax savings and financial benefits for you and/or your beneficiaries. While your primary motivation for giving should be philanthropic, a trust's benefits can make that altruism less dear. In some cases, much of the money given through a trust is funds the tax collector would have staked large claims on anyhow. So why not direct the money to something you can feel passionate about? The following trusts are set up for tax benefits and charitable giving.

Charitable Remainder Trust. A charitable remainder trust (CRT) provides income to an individual and/or one or more other designated beneficiaries for the rest of their life or a maximum of twenty years. After that time limit (or life) expires, the trust's principal is distributed to a charity. The reasons for doing this—aside from the obvious benefit it will eventually have for the charity—is that it gives immediate income tax deductions, reduces the size of your estate, and offers the possibility of putting the full value of an appreciated asset to work generating income (for you or a beneficiary).

Let's say, for example, that you had bet $5,000 on Bill Gates and his Microsoft cronies ten years ago and those shares have grown to $415,000. You want to share your good fortune, but as your other stocks didn't fare so well, you need income from that windfall. If you sold Microsoft (which doesn't pay a dividend), you'd generate a tax bill of $82,000. But if you put the stock into a charitable trust and then sold it, you could put the full $415,000 to work throwing off income, *plus* get a sizable tax deduction.

There are two basic types of CRTs: the charitable remainder unitrust and charitable remainder annuity trust. The remainder annuity trust pays a fixed, guaranteed amount each year; unitrust payments are based on a set percentage of the trust's annual market value.

There is plenty of flexibility within a remainder trust: you can invest in stocks and not use the profits and income for years; you can have the income held until it's time to pay for your grandchildren's education; or you could give a portion of the trust's income to your children. They, in turn, could use that money to purchase insurance on your life to replace the value of the inheritance that went to charity.

To receive current tax deductions and exclude the value of the remainder trust from one's estate, the irrevocable gift must be made while you're still alive. Trusts that take effect only upon death offer limited tax benefits.

Charitable trusts can be funded with almost any property, including real estate or privately held stock. Most charitable remainder trusts require at least $100,000, although some charities will set them up for $50,000.

Charitable Lead Trust. A charitable lead trust is for those who don't need the income from their investments themselves but don't want to deny their heirs the principal. Basically, it's the opposite of the remainder trust, in that the charity uses the income from your gift, but when the giver dies, the principal goes to the donor's *non*charitable beneficiaries.

Charitable lead trusts can significantly reduce gift and estate taxes. The donor is essentially trading tax deductions for herself now for tax savings for her heirs later. Charitable lead trusts generally don't create immediate tax deductions, but after a lead trust is established, the value of the gift is no longer included in a taxable estate. Yet upon death (or the end of the trust term), when the property returns to noncharitable beneficiaries, it is often at an increased value— even after taxes. The tax calculations for charitable lead trusts can get complicated, so they should only be considered after consultation with a qualified estate and tax professional.

FOR SHALLOWER POCKETS

Charitable Gift Annuity. A charitable gift annuity is easy to confuse with a charitable remainder annuity trust, since their names are so similar and the two do basically the same job: the principal from your gift generates a guaranteed income for the designated noncharitable individual(s) and goes to the charity when you die or the annuity expires. Both work well with appreciated assets that haven't been taxed yet.

The legal difference between the gift annuity and remainder annuity trust is that gift annuities are backed by the assets of the charitable organization, not by the trust itself. The functional difference[4] for a donor lies in the minimums (gift annuities typically start at $10,000), the limitations on property that can fund it (no privately held stock for gift annuities), and their tax treatment.

As with remainder trusts, donations to a gift annuity receive immediate tax deductions. In the case of the gift annuity, however, the deduction is based on the difference between the purchase price of the annuity and the value of the annuity payments (calculated using actuarial tables). As with the remainder trust, you must pay income taxes on payments received, but for gift annuities a portion of that income is tax-free. If appreciated property is used to fund a gift annuity, no immediate capital gains tax is due, but you do ultimately have to pay tax on those gains; that tax liability is just spread out over the donor's life expectancy.

If this sounds confusing, it's because it is. You're navigating within tax rulings that have been created partly from legislation and partly from legal cases tried in the courts. To get a better sense of the type of giving that works for you, contact

---

4. The fact that a charitable gift annuity is backed by the charity instead of the assets in a trust can be nervous-making for those concerned about the non-profit's being sued or grossly mismanaged. Most states have precautions in place against those possibilities. If this consideration concerns you, ask the charity you're considering donating to for details about regulations in its state.

one of the charitable groups you're interested in and have it do the calculations for you. Large nonprofits have planned-giving departments that would be happy to assist you, illustrate some numbers, and answer questions free of charge.

The annual payments from your gift annuity depend on your age when you make the gift. In many cases it makes sense to defer the income. Let's say you're a forty- or fifty-something donor in a high tax bracket. You can take a tax write-off now, when you really need it, and defer receiving the income until retirement, when you'll most likely be in a lower income tax bracket.

Pooled Income Fund. A pooled income fund is a common trust that allows gifts from many donors to be combined for investment purposes. Pooled income funds can be funded with as little as $5,000 (in cash or stocks only). The income such a fund pays will vary from year to year because pooled income funds are invested in stocks and bonds. As with any mutual fund, its payout will vary according to the portfolio's performance. Appreciated stock donated to a pooled income fund fully bypasses capital gains taxes, but all your payments are fully taxable as ordinary income.

ON DEATH AND RETIREMENT PLANS: A LARGE TAX MAN COMETH

Know all that money you've been so carefully socking away for a rainy day in your IRA, Keogh, or 401(k) plan? Well, if you did too good a job and keel over tomorrow, between income, state, and estate taxes, the IRS could glom on to as much as 75 percent of it. You see, the feds gave us a tax-free, or deductible, ride going into retirement accounts, but they make darn sure someone pays the toll on the way out. Income tax must be paid on those savings when they're used—whether it comes out of your pocket or your beneficiary's. (Distributions from Roth IRAs aren't taxable. See pages 73–74 for details.) The only exception is when your beneficiary is a charity.

There are no estate taxes on retirement funds when you die with less than $650,000 in assets, but if you're over that amount, the combination of income and estate taxes makes retirement funds excellent charitable gifts. This allows all your savings to go to something meaningful to you, instead of the IRS's taking the lion's share of it—or at the very least, 48 percent.

A SMALL CONFESSION AND
A FEW REMINDERS

A holistic approach to money marries our inner and outer life, uniting our feelings, values, and hopes with the world of commerce. As with any good marriage, it takes wisdom, skill, and compromise to really work; and mishaps and missteps are to be expected. After all, even the best marriages have their moments.

I'll be the first to admit (or maybe the second, after my wife) that I don't have the money thing mastered. I'm not beyond whining about the price of gifts, wincing when making charitable donations, or withering at the cost of a family vacation. I have a ways to go before becoming a paradigm of money health.

I am, however, improving. Writing this book has helped my relationship to money. I've simplified my finances and become comfortable paying more for sustainably produced, healthy foods and products. (I was already pretty good at the budgeting and investing end of things.) More important, I've relaxed money's grip on my emotions. My spending discomfort and financial worries have decreased in frequency and intensity; I've gone from knowing the "right" way to be to mostly living it—often only later realizing that similar situations in the past would have caused me to struggle.

That said, I don't expect to be free of money worries anytime soon; that isn't even my goal. Of course, being worry-free would be nice but making that my aim creates its own problems: in my desire to "succeed," I tend to dismiss or ignore negative emotions—which only buries them. What works better is being aware of any worry, fear, or discomfort that accompanies money matters; by fully experiencing these, without trying to push them away, I usually find that I understand my feelings better and that they weren't so bad after all. As with letting light into a basement, once you can see down there, things aren't as scary as you thought—and any mold that was growing dies naturally.

Real change takes more than just willpower. It takes time, doggedness, and finesse. As I've noted elsewhere, true money mastery isn't a destination but an ongoing challenge. Improvements rarely unfold in a straight line, and expecting an easy makeover only makes one more likely to crumble in the face of real obstacles. Instead of giving answers, *The Mindful Money Guide* offers tools and direction.

We all have financial setbacks—even if we've done our homework and have the best of intentions. The stock market might plunge, washing away much of your nest egg; you may be faced with a financially debilitating divorce; or more likely, you'll get caught by an everyday handwringer, such as needing a new transmission just after writing a check to your daughter's camp which you can scarcely afford.

When you're thrown for a financial loop, the following thoughts can give perspective. They probably won't come as news to you, but if you're like me, you can never really hear them too often—especially when feeling frazzled.

- When fretting about financial matters, remember that one of the reasons you want money in the first place is for peace of mind. By worrying about money, you undermine what you're actually after. This is especially good to remember when you're upset over a loss that doesn't really affect your day-to-day situation. Savings are meant for absorbing unexpected expenses and financial setbacks without disrupting your life. Getting into a tizzy about a small misfortune undermines the whole point of having any fortune.

- Accept the present moment. Whether your current financial situation or problem is "meant to be" or not, responding as if that were the case—as if each situation had something to teach us—is the healthiest way to live. "Be here now" is another way of saying, "Face the truth as it arises." The mental gymnastics we perform to avoid what's right in front of us usually cause more pain and anguish than events themselves.

   Accepting the way things are doesn't mean being passive; it means being open. And openness actually fosters an increased responsiveness: once you drop wishful thinking and resistance to the situation at hand, appropriate action will often seem obvious and intuitive.

- Our head and our cash should be in the service of our heart—not the other way around. Since our culture emphasizes bottom-line results and rational thinking, it's easy to forget that feelings matter most. This isn't a New Age excuse to discard rationality but a reminder about priorities.

- Carve your own path. It's not easy to say no to cell phones and the Internet when everyone else is signing on; it can be hard to stay with a low-paying (but rewarding) job when your neighbor uses her bonus to install a movie-quality home theater and take a winter vacation in Hawaii.

Candid Camera once did an episode in which a doctor's waiting room was filled with stooge patients wearing only underwear. When new, real patients came in, they, too, would disrobe, without even asking why. In that situation, the herd instinct is comical, but when you think about the implications for our own lives—the difficulty we have in following our own intuition and common sense—it's more scary or sad than amusing.

Too often we live for what we imagine others want or expect of us. Motivated by cultural archetypes or family expectations, we override our truest feelings. As psychologist Karen Horney put it, we suffer from "the tyranny of the should."

Comparing yourself with others is a losing game—yet it's hard to resist. If you find yourself feeling jealous of someone else's cash position, at least try to think in terms of the person's whole life: How content is this person you're envying? And if he is happy, is it because of his money?

• Focus on the difference between money and wealth. It's easy to forget that a true accounting of your wealth includes intangible assets such as friends, family, health, energy level, and overall state of mind.

The twelfth-century Jewish sage Moses Maimonides noted that the things we need the most—starting with air, water, and food—are the most abundant and that most of our unhappiness is caused by wanting things that aren't necessary.

• Mistakes are part of life. As parents, we tell our kids this time and again, yet we always seem to forget it ourselves. It's hard to shake what was drilled into us in school (and possibly at home)—that we must get *the* right answer.

Real life, of course, is more about choices and shades of gray. Trying to choose *the* correct answer is usually a mistake, born from thinking of the world "out there" as a fixed entity rather than a process in motion.

For an investment, a business venture, or a new job to work out as we hope, many factors beyond our control must contribute. Thinking through "as if" scenarios should be part of decision making, but even the biggest brain can't anticipate all possible variables.

The most important part of any decision-making process is clarifying your values. Every pros-and-cons list should be trumped by your highest value. You may, for example, be considering an appealing job that entails moving to California. Despite looking forward to the work and weather, if being near your family and friends in Cincinnati is more important, stay in Ohio. We can't ultimately know how things will work out before making a decision, but at least we can know we did the right thing according to our own lights.

When I make a bad decision, I often focus on what I've lost. But as time passes, the loss rarely matters; it's my behavior at the time that is more likely to bother me. My biggest regrets aren't about outcomes but about acting without courage, dignity, sensitivity, or well-considered reasoning. Mistakes are learning opportunities. When reviewing them, it's better to focus on how we reached the decision instead of thinking about how things should be different.

And finally, remember that the future is now. By that I don't mean, as the mystic does, that we should live in the eternal present (although that can only help); rather, it's a simple reminder that there is no better time to live fully and with integrity than right now.

Since life rarely unfolds just as we want, we often fall into imagining how it or we could be different. What these fantasies distract us from (besides what's happening right under our noses) is that unless *we* change, things can't truly be much different. Striking it rich may get us a better car, house, or job, but that won't change who we are. If you were bored with your cottage, you'll soon tire of your mansion. And if you were stingy on a modest salary, you won't be generous-hearted as a multimillionaire—even if you send $1,000 checks to charity. As Marcel Proust observed, "The real voyage of discovery consists not in seeing new landscapes, but in having new eyes."

There is no better time to live well. No better time to be kind, thoughtful, and not let money run your life. If we picture that happening when our ship comes in, look again— and ask what will really be so different then.

APPENDIX

PERSONAL FINANCE

A NOTE ABOUT BOOKKEEPING

The fewer financial accounts you have the better. It means less paperwork to file, less statements to check, and less addresses to change should you move. Some investments, such as DRIPS (dividend reinvestment programs) sound appealing because they let the "little" guy/gal get started investing, but they create more paperwork than an unpaid Manhattan parking ticket.

BANKS & BANKING-RELATED GROUPS

CANICCOR, PO Box 426829, San Francisco, CA 94142. 415-885-5102. A banking watchdog group.

Creative Investment Research, PO Box 55793, Washington, DC 20040. 202-722-5000. Surveys and evaluates information from women- and minority-owned banks.

National Federation of Community Development Credit Unions, 120 Wall St., 10th fl., New York, NY 10005. 212-809-1850. The national association of credit unions that serve low-income communities.

The National Bankers Association, 1802 T St. NW, Washington, DC 20009. 202-588-5432. Offers a list of "speciality banks." The abbreviated list below can get you started in the meantime.

SOME SOCIALLY RESPONSIBLE
BANKS AND CREDIT UNIONS

Albina Community Bank, 2002 NE Martin Luther King Blvd., Portland, OR 97217. 503-288-7286. Albina focuses on ensuring that minorities, women, and low-to-middle-income borrowers are serviced.

Alternatives Federal Credit Union, 301 W. State St., Ithaca, NY 14850. 607-273-4666.

Bank Boston/First Community Bank, 100 Federal St., Boston, MA 02110. 800-788-5000.

Bank of Newport, 1000 SW Broadway, Suite 1100, Portland, OR 97205. 503-224-4245.

Blackfeet National Bank, PO Box 730, Browning, MT 59417. 406-338-7000.

Community Bank of the Bay, 1750 Broadway, Oakland, CA 94612. 510-271-8400.

Community Capital Bank, 111 Livingston St., Brooklyn, NY 11201. 718-802-1212.

Elk Horn Bank and Trust, 601 Main St., Arkadelphia, AR 71923. 800-789-3428.

NCB Savings Bank, 139 High St., Hillsboro, OH 45133. 800-322-1251.

Self-Help Credit Union, PO Box 3619, Durham, NC 27702. 800-966-7353.

South Shore Bank, 7054 S. Jeffrey Blvd., Chicago, IL 60649. 800-669-7725.

ShoreBank Pacific. 800-669-7725. The nation's first fully environmentally focused bank.

Vermont National, PO Box 804, Brattleboro, VT 05302. 800-772-3863.

Wainwright Bank & Trust Company, 63 Franklin St., Boston, MA 02110. 800-444-BANK.

Women's World Banking, 8 W. 20th St., 10th fl., New York, NY 10018. 212-768-8513.

CHECKS

The following companies offer environmentally friendly checks (the last three for considerably less than at most banks):

Message! Products. 800-243-2565.

Check Gallery. 800-354-3540.

Current Checks. 800-533-3973.

The Check Store. 800-424-3257.

INSURANCE

The following companies offer low rates on term life insurance:

Quotesmith. 800-431-1147. www.quotesmith.com

Wholesale Insurance Network. 800-808-5810.

Insurance Quote Services. 800-972-1104.

Automated Life Insurance Quotation Systems. 800-400-4832.

Ameritas Low-Load. 800-552-3553.

USAA. 800-531-8000.

Insurance Information. 800-472-5800. Does comparison shopping for you but doesn't offer policies directly.

COMMODITY INDEX FUND

At the time of this writing, Oppenheimer's Real Asset Fund (800-525-7048) is the first and only readily available commodity index fund in the United States. Imitators with lower fees may follow.

CDs VS. TREASURY BONDS

One possible advantage Treasury notes and bonds have over CDs is they are salable if you want the money before it comes due. This, however, is helpful only when interest rates have dropped. Otherwise—between commissions and lower bond prices—the small penalty for an early withdrawal from a CD should be less than the loss from selling your Treasuries. (Although penalties vary from bank to bank, typical early withdrawal penalties are 3 or 6 months' worth of interest.)

GNMA DETAILS

Vanguard (800-635-1511) offers a well-performing no-commission GNMA fund that has the lowest expense ratio around.

BOND FUNDS

After buying CDs, mutual funds are the easiest—although not necessarily the savviest—way to buy bonds. Minimums are small and your only real effort is in deciding which fund to go with. Once you've done that, professional investors make all the buying, researching, and selling decisions for you. This of course doesn't ensure profits: the price of a fund will still fluctuate inversely to interest rates and since there is no maturity date on the fund, there is never a guarantee of getting all your investment back—though if you reinvest your income for a few years, you probably won't lose money unless interest rates skyrocket.

As a general rule, a no-commission fund with the lowest expense ratio is your best bet (Vanguard tends to be king of the no-loads with slim management fees. 800-635-1511). A bond investing star à la Peter Lynch or Warren Buffett has never emerged, so you don't need to do vigorous research. Over time, most bond funds tend to perform about the same as their associates, thus the importance of looking for a fund with low fees.

Do note, however, if you're willing to put a little effort in, outside of convenience and low minimums, there isn't much reason to buy a bond fund. Bonds are safer than stocks and have fewer moving parts. Diversification isn't nearly as important as it is for equities—especially for municipal and government bonds that are already guaranteed. So if you don't mind the little extra effort of choosing your own bonds, you can boost your returns by avoiding the fees and commissions usually associated with buying bond funds and unit trusts (an inactive fund which typically charges 4 or 5 percent commission).

TAX-FREE BOND FUNDS

There are a handful of tax-free mutual funds, marketed as socially responsible, which buy bonds seeking socially positive projects, like pollution control, public transportation, school construction, or wastewater improvement. Parnassus (800-999-3505) and Citizens Trust (800-223-7010) have no-commission SRI tax-free funds that buy California municipal bonds. Calvert Group (800-368-2748) has seven state-specific funds (CA, NY, PA, MI, MD, VA, VT), but they come with an initial 3.75 percent sales commission. If you feel comfortable with general-issue municipal bonds (i.e., you feel fine with however the state of, say, Connecticut or Wisconsin spends its money), then the Vanguard Group (800-635-1511) generally has the least expensive and best performing bond funds.

RECOMMENDED SRI STOCK MUTUAL FUNDS

The Domini Social Equity Fund. 800-762-6814. $1,000 minimum.

Citizens Trust Index. 800-223-7010. $2,500 minimum.

The Green Century Equity Fund. 800-934-7336. $2,000 minimum.

DEVCAP. 800-371-2655. $1,000 minimum.

Ariel Appreciation. 800-725-0140. $1,000 minimum.

Pax World Balanced. 800-767-1729. $250 minimum.

RECOMMENDED AGGRESSIVE STOCK MUTUAL FUNDS (NON-SRI)

What follows are the best funds in each sector with the lowest fees. Within each grouping I've listed the fund in long-term performance order, from best to runners-up—all are no-load funds unless noted. All have handily beat the S&P 500.

Health Care:

Vanguard Specialized Health Care. 800-662-7447.

Fidelity Select Health Care. 800-544-8888. 3% load.

Invesco Strategic Health Sciences. 800-525-8085.

Technology funds:

Fidelity Select Electronic and Fidelity Select Computers. 800-544-8888. 3% load.

T. Rowe Price Science & Technology. 800-638-5660.

Invesco Strategic Technology. 800-525-8085.

BOOKS FOR LEARNING STOCK-PICKING SKILLS

Lynch, Peter and John Rothchild. *One Up on Wall Street: How to Use What You Already Know to Make Money in the Market.* New York: Penguin Books, 1990.

Rosenberg, Claude N. *Stock Market Primer.* New York: Warner Books, 1987.

Train, John. *The Money Masters.* New York: Penguin Books, 1980.

Graham, Benjamin. *The Intelligent Investor.* New York: Harper-Collins, 4th rev. ed. 1985.

EXCLUSIVE SRI BROKER

First Affirmative Financial Network. 800-422-7284.

SHAREHOLDER ACTIVISM

Interfaith Center on Corporate Responsibility, 475 Riverside Dr., Rm. 550, New York, New York 10115. 212-870-2295. info@iccr.org

Investor Responsibility Research Center, 1350 Connecticut Ave. NW, Washington, DC 20036. 202-833-0700. www.irrc.org

REITs

The following REITs have performed well and invest in properties you can feel good about. There are many more REITs available that invest in health-care facilities and nursing homes. Before investing get an annual report, news releases, and check out the company's 10-k to see what they're currently working on.

Rouse Properties, 10275 Little Patuxet Pkwy., Columbia, MD 21044. 410-992-6000.

CRIIMI MAE Inc., 11200 Rockville Pike, Rockville, MD 20852. 800-CMM-0535.

Health Care Property Investors, Inc., 10990 Wilshire Blvd., Suite 1200, Los Angeles, CA 90024. 310-473-1990.

Healthcare Realty Trust, 3310 West End Avenue, Suite 400, Nashville, TN 37203. 615-269-8175. NYSE: HR.

TAX CREDIT LIMITED PARTNERSHIPS

The following general partners have good long-term track records:

Boston Capital Tax Credit Funds, Boston Capital Services, Inc., 1 Boston Plaza, Boston, MA 02108-4406. 617-624-8900. 800-955-2733.

WNC Housing Tax Credit Funds, 3158 Redhill Avenue, Suite 120, Costa Mesa, CA 92626-3416. 714-662-5565. 800-451-7070.

FOR ROTH VS. REGULAR IRA CALCULATIONS

T. Rowe Price (www.troweprice.com) or the Strong funds (www.strong-funds.com). Both have retirement calculators that can quickly crunch numbers for you.

FINANCING COLLEGE

FINANCIAL AID

There are no simple and accurate formulas for projecting how much colleges will expect you to contribute to your child's education—and offers will vary greatly from school to school. But a rough guideline (based on 1997 dollars) is that as household income goes above $50,000, the amount of aid you're likely to get drops significantly.

The chart below gives ballpark estimates of how much financial aid will cover. It's impossible to project exactly—as not only do schools use different formulas, the same university may offer different aid packages depending on how badly it wants the student and how it has already allocated other money.

HOW MUCH WILL FINANCIAL AID COVER TODAY?

ESTIMATED PERCENTAGE OF AVERAGE PUBLIC AND PRIVATE COLLEGE COSTS PAID FOR BY FINANCIAL AID

ANNUAL FAMILY PRETAX INCOME

TOTAL FAMILY ASSETS*	$30,000 PUBLIC	PRIVATE	$50,000 PUBLIC	PRIVATE	$70,000 PUBLIC	PRIVATE	$90,000 PUBLIC	PRIVATE
$20,000	80%	91%	53%	78%	0%	47%	0%	20%
40,000	80	91	53	78	0	47	0	20
60,000	75	88	33	69	0	40	0	15
80,000	70	86	24	64	0	37	0	9
100,000	69	85	12	58	0	31	0	4

*DOES NOT INCLUDE EQUITY IN HOME.

NOTE: THE PERCENTAGE OF COLLEGE COSTS COVERED BY FINANCIAL AID ARE BASED ON APPROXIMATE EXPECTED PARENTAL CONTRIBUTIONS TOWARD 1997–98 COLLEGE EXPENSES (FOR A FAMILY OF FOUR, WITH NO OTHER FAMILY MEMBERS ATTENDING COLLEGE) FROM *PETERSON'S GUIDE TO FOUR-YEAR COLLEGES 1997*, AND WERE CALCULATED USING THE COLLEGE BOARD'S AVERAGE, COMPREHENSIVE PUBLIC COLLEGE COST OF $10,069 AND PRIVATE COLLEGE COST OF $21,424 FOR 1997–98.

SOURCE: T. ROWE PRICE (REPRINTED WITH PERMISSION)

INTERNET HELP

There are several Web sites on the Internet that will let you plug in your financial data and then automatically give you aid projections. The category killer site for financial aid formulas, or for any financial aid concern for that matter, is the Financial Aid Information Page: www.finaid.org

CO-OP EDUCATION PROGRAMS

For more information, contact the Center for Co-operative Education, Northeastern University, 503 Sterns, Boston, MA 02115. 617-373-2000

SPENDING IT

To be more knowledgeable about the products you buy read *The Green Consumer* by Joel Makower and *Stuff: The Secret Lives of Everyday Things* by Alan Thein Durning. Subscribing to *Co-op America Quarterly* (202-872-5307), the *Green Guide* (888-ECO-INFO), or *Green Living* (802-348-7441) can help keep you up-to-date on the environmental life (and afterlife) of the goods we buy.

To get a sense of which large companies are the most progressive, fair, and environmentally sensitive, get publications put out by the Council on Economic Priorities (800-729-4237). Its most famous book, *Shopping for a Better World,* rates America's largest corporations on eight criteria—from environmental impact and opportunities for women and minorities to charitable giving and community outreach.

TO START A CAR CO-OP

The kit costs $50 and can be ordered from RAIN, PO Box 30097, Eugene, OR 97403.

The best Web site on the topic is www.eagletree.com/think.can

USED CARS

Edmund's New Cars: Prices & Reviews gives price information and fair values for every kind of used car you can think of. www.edmunds.com

TO START YOUR OWN FOOD CO-OP

For more details, contact the Co-operative Development Services (608-258-4396), which offers a brochure on starting a co-op. Center for Co-operatives (608-262-3981) has an extensive library on co-ops, and NCBA (202-632-6222) has a video on starting a buying club.

FOR A CSA

To find a CSA near you, send a self-addressed, stamped envelope to Community Supported Agriculture of North America, Indian Line Farm, 57 Jugend Road, Great Barrington, MA 01230. For biodynamic CSA farms call 800-516-7797.

BOYCOTTS

To keep up on the latest boycott news, get *Co-op America Quarterly* ($20 per year; 202-872-5307), which includes *Boycott Action News*, a convenient-for-shopping pull-out section. *Boycott Action News* is produced in conjunction with *Boycott Quarterly*, which has even more extensive boycott listings and information (PO Box 30727, Seattle, WA 98103; $20 per year). If you're up for organizing your own boycott, send for *Co-op America*'s "Boycott Organizer's Guide" ($2), which tells you how to do it right.

CREDIT CARDS

Working Assets. 800-788-8588.

MBNA (800-847-7378) and First USA (800-FIRST-USA) can tell you which nonprofit groups they have programs with.

RESOURCES FOR COUNTERACTING MARKETING ONSLAUGHT

Media Foundation. 800-663-1243. Publisher of *Adbusters Quarterly*. www.adbusters.org

For a detailed list of all the organizations you need to contact to totally prevent junk mail from reaching you, get the $3 booklet *Stop Junk Mail Forever* from Good Advice Press, PO Box 78, Elizaville, NY 12523.

To keep up with and employ the latest and greatest commercial defense techniques, visit anti-junk mail Web sites like Electronic Privacy Information Center (www. epic.com) or www.obviously.com/junkmail. These can give you more sophisticated techniques like installing a mail filter (www.axxis.com) or using a remailer. To find more Web sites on the topic, type in the terms "spam" or "junk e-mail" to a browser and follow the most promising leads.

COOKIE CRUMBLER SOFTWARE

As of this writing there are only a few programs which allow users to prevent cookies from being stored in their browsers, but rest assured that more are on the way.

Free programs (some are delayed versions that are mainly to sell you their faster versions) that allow anonymous Internet surfing:

The Anonymizer, which not only blocks cookies but prevents any information about your browser, IP address, or computer platform from being released, is available at www.anonymizer.com

Luckman's Anonymous Cookie for Internet Privacy™ is at www.luckman.com

Pretty Good Privacy, Inc., has a modestly priced product called PGP-cookie.cutter that allows users to selectively block cookies from specific sites, while allowing other cookies to pass through.

NetAngels can block cookies as part of a larger service to point users toward "affinity" Web sites that match their interests.

EARNING IT

The following books are helpful for investigating personality type systems:

Do What You Are: Discover the Perfect Career for You Through the Secrets of Personality Type by Paul Tieger and Barbara Barron-Tieger uses the Myers-Briggs system to help you uncover your ideal work. It asks you to consider where you fall on four dimensions of personality assessment (Extroversion-Introversion, Sensing-Intuition, Thinking-Feeling, Judging-Perceiving). Based on those determinations, it presents a variety of careers that would work for you and explains why.

Personality Types: Using the Enneagram for Self-Discovery by Don Riso and *The Enneagram* by Helen Palmer are excellent introductions to this ancient, Sufi-based system. Helen Palmer's *The Enneagram in Love and Work* addresses some work issues directly.

BIBLIOGRAPHY

Anderson, Nancy. *Work with Passion: How to Do What You Love for a Living.* New York: Carroll & Graf Publishers, 1984.

Applegarth, Ginger. *The Money Diet: Reaping the Rewards of Financial Fitness.* New York: Penguin Books, 1995.

Ashton, Debra. *The Complete Guide to Planned Giving.* Cambridge, Mass.: JLA Publications, 1988.

Berg, Adriane B. *Your Kids, Your Money.* Englewood Cliffs, N.J.: Prentice-Hall, 1985.

Berthold-Bond, Annie. *The Green Kitchen Handbook.* New York: HarperPerennial, 1997.

Bloom, William. *Money, Heart, and Mind: Financial Well-Being for People and the Planet.* London: Penguin Group, 1995.

Blumstein, Philip, and Pepper Schwartz. *American Couples: Money, Work, Sex.* New York: Simon & Schuster, 1985.

Bobo, Kim, Jackie Kendall, and Steve Max. *Organize! A Manual for Activists in the 1990s.* Cabin John, Md.: Seven Locks Press, 1991.

Bodnar, Janet. *Money-Smart Kids.* Washington, D.C.: Kiplinger Books, 1993.

Boldt, Laurence. *Zen and the Art of Making a Living: A Practical Guide to Creative Career Design.* New York: Penguin Arkana, 1993.

Bolles, Richard. *What Color Is Your Parachute?* Berkeley, Calif.: Ten Speed Press, 1988.

Breen, T. H. "The Truth about Gentle Ben." *The New York Times Book Review,* September 22, 1996, p. 37.

Brill, Jack, and Alan Reder. *Investing from the Heart: The Guide to Socially Responsible Investments and Money Management.* New York: Crown Publishers, 1992.

Bryan, Mark, and Julia Cameron. *The Money Drunk: 90 Days to Financial Freedom.* New York: Ballantine Books, 1992.

Buchan, James. *Frozen Desire: The Meaning of Money.* New York: Farrar Straus & Giroux, 1997.

Cameron, Julia, and Mark Bryan. *The Artist's Way: A Spiritual Path to Higher Creativity.* New York: Putnam, 1992.

Carter, Stephen, and Julia Sokol. *Lives without Balance: When You're Giving Everything You've Got and Still Not Getting What You Hoped For.* New York: Villard Books, 1992.

Chapman, Jack, and Steve Sanders. *How to Make $1,000 a Minute: Negotiating Your Salaries and Raises.* Berkeley, Calif.: Ten Speed Press, 1987.

Chodron, Pema. *Start Where You Are: A Guide to Compassionate Living.* Boston: Shambhala Publications, 1994.

Clason, George. *The Richest Man in Babylon.* New York: Hawthorn/Dutton, 1955.

Clifford, Denis. *Nolo's Simple Will Book: How to Prepare a Legally Valid Will.* Berkeley, Calif.: Nolo Press, 1987.

————. *Plan Your Estate with a Living Trust.* Berkeley, Calif.: Nolo Press, 1992.

Coles, Robert. *The Call of Service: A Witness to Idealism.* Boston: Houghton Mifflin, 1992.

Council for Economic Priorities. *Shopping for a Better World: The Quick and Easy Guide to All Your Socially Responsible Shopping.* San Francisco: Sierra Club Books, 1994.

Covey, Stephen. *The Seven Habits of Highly Effective People: Powerful Lessons in Personal Change.* New York: Simon & Schuster, 1989.

Curry, Hayden, Denis Clifford, and Robin Leopnard. *A Legal Guide for Lesbian and Gay Couples.* Berkeley, Calif.: Nolo Press, 1994.

Dass, Ram, and Mirabai Bush. *Compassion in Action: Setting Out on the Path of Service.* New York: Bell Tower, 1992.

Dass, Ram, and Paul Gorman. *How Can I Help? Stories and Reflections on Service.* New York: Knopf, 1985.

Dominguez, Joe, and Vicki Robin. *Your Money or Your Life: Transforming Your Relationship with Money and Achieving Financial Independence.* New York: Viking, 1992.

Drucker, Peter. *Managing the Non-Profit Organization: Principles and Practices.* New York: HarperBusiness, 1990.

Dunn, Thomas. *How to Shake the New Money Tree: Creative Fundraising for Nonprofit Organizations.* New York: Penguin, 1988.

Durning, Alan. *How Much Is Enough: The Consumer Society and the Future of the Earth.* New York: Norton, 1992.

Dyer, Wayne W. *The Sky's the Limit.* New York: Simon & Schuster, 1980.

Elgin, Duane. *Voluntary Simplicity: Toward a Way of Life That Is Outwardly Simple, Inwardly Rich.* New York: Quill/William Morrow, 1993.

Felton-Collins, Victoria. *Couples and Money: Why Money Interferes with Love and What to Do about It.* New York: Bantam, 1990.

Flanagan, Joan. *The Successful Volunteer Organization: Getting Started and Getting Results in Nonprofit Charitable, Grass Roots, and Community Groups.* Chicago: Contemporary Books, 1984.

Fox, Matthew. *The Reinvention of Work: A New Vision of Livelihood in Our Time.* San Francisco: HarperSanFrancisco, 1994.

Gawain, Shakti. *Creative Visualization.* Mill Valley, Calif.: Whatever Publishing, 1981.

Geever, Jane, and Patricia McNeill. *The Foundation Center's Guide to Proposal Writing.* New York: Foundation Center, 1993.

Goldbeck, David, and Nikki Goldbeck. *Choose to Reuse: An Encyclopedia of Services, Products, Programs, and Charitable Organizations That Foster Reuse.* Woodstock, N.Y.: Ceres Press, 1995.

Green, Mark. *The Consumer Bible: 1001 Ways to Shop Smart.* New York: Workman Publishing, 1995.

Harman, Willis, and Howard Rheingold. *Higher Creativity: Liberating the Unconscious for Breakthrough Insights.* Los Angeles: Jeremy Tarcher, 1984.

Hawken, Paul. *Growing a Business.* New York: Simon & Schuster, 1987.

Hazel Henderson. *Building a Win-Win World.* San Francisco: Berret-Koehler Publishers, 1996.

Hillman, James. *The Soul's Code: In Search of Character and Calling.* New York: Random House, 1996.

Hollender, Jeffrey. *How to Make the World a Better Place: A Guide to Doing Good.* New York: Quill/William Morrow, 1990.

Hyde, Lewis. *The Gift.* New York: Random House, 1983.

Ihara, Tony, and Ralph Warner. *The Living Together Kit: A Legal Guide for Unmarried Couples.* Berkeley, Calif.: Nolo Press, 1994.

Johnson, Paul. *A History of Christianity.* New York: Atheneum, 1976.

Kano, Susan. *Making Peace with Food: A Step-by-Step Guide to Freedom from Diet/Weight Conflict.* Canbury, Conn.: Amity Publishing, 1985.

Levering, Robert. *A Great Place to Work: What Makes Some Employers So Good (and Most So Bad).* New York: Random House, 1988.

Lockhart, Russell. *Soul and Money.* Dallas: Spring Publications, 1982.

Loeb, Marshall. *Marshall Loeb's 1994 Money Guide.* Boston: Little, Brown, 1993.

Lowry, Ritchie. *Good Money: A Guide to Profitable Social Investing in the '90s.* New York: Norton, 1991.

Luks, Allan, and Peggy Payne. *The Healing Power of Doing Good.* New York: Fawcett Columbine, 1992.

Lynch, Peter. *One Up on Wall Street: How to Use What You Already Know to Make Money in the Market.* New York: Penguin Books, 1990.

Makower, Joel. *The Green Consumer.* New York: Penguin Books, 1993.

Mander, Jerry. *In the Absence of the Sacred: The Failure of Technology and the Survival of the Indian Nations.* San Francisco: Sierra Club Books, 1992.

McKibben, Bill. *Maybe One: A Personal and Environmental Argument for Single-Child Families.* New York: Simon & Schuster, 1998.

Mellon, Olivia. *Money Harmony: Resolving Money Conflicts in Your Life and Relationships.* New York: Walker & Company, 1994.

Miller, Timothy. *How to Want What You Have: Discovering the Magic and Grandeur of Ordinary Existence.* New York: Henry Holt, 1996.

Mogil, Christopher, Anne Slepian, and Peter Woodrow. *They Gave Away a Fortune: Stories of People Who Have Devoted Themselves and Their Wealth to Peace, Justice, and the Environment.* Philadelphia, Pa.: New Society Publishers, 1992.

Needleman, Jacob. *Money and the Meaning of Life.* New York: Doubleday Currency, 1994.

Nolo Press. *Nolo's Everyday Law Book.* Berkeley, Calif.: Nolo Press, 1997.

Palmer, Helen. *The Enneagram.* San Francisco: HarperSanFrancisco, 1991.

———. *The Enneagram in Love and Work: Understanding Your Intimate and Business Relationships.* San Francisco: HarperCollins West, 1995.

Pinker, Steven. *How the Mind Works.* New York: Norton, 1997.

Pond, Jonathan. *The New Century Family Money Book: Your Comprehensive Guide to a Lifetime of Financial Security.* New York: Dell, 1993.

Ray, Sondra. *The Only Diet There Is.* Berkeley, Calif.: Celestial Arts, 1981.

Riso, Don Richard. *Personality Types: Using the Enneagram for Self-Discovery.* Boston: Houghton Mifflin, 1987.

Robbins, Anthony. *Awaken the Giant Within.* New York: Summit Books, 1991.

Rosenberg, Claude. *Stock Market Primer.* New York: Warner Books, 1987.

———. *Wealthy and Wise: How You and America Can Get the Most Out of Your Giving.* Boston: Little, Brown, 1994.

Ryan, John C., and Alan Thein Durning. *Stuff: The Secret Lives of Everyday Things.* Seattle: Northwest Environmental Watch, 1997.

Schor, Juliet B. *The Overworked American.* New York: Basic Books, 1994.

Schwartz, Tony. *What Really Matters: Searching for Wisdom in America.* New York: Bantam, 1995.

Seligman, Martin. *What You Can Change and What You Can't.* New York: Knopf, 1993.

Sheimo, Michael. *Stock Market Rules: 50 of the Most Widely Held Investment Axioms Explained, Examined, and Exposed.* Chicago: Probus Publishing, 1994.

Shi, David. *The Simple Life: Plain Living and High Thinking in American Culture.* New York: Oxford University Press, 1985.

Sinetar, Marsha. *Work as a Spiritual Practice: How to Bring Joy and Meaning to Your Work Life.* Audiotape. Boulder, Colo.: Sounds True Recordings, 1992.

Slepian, Anne, and Christopher Mogil. *Welcome to Philanthropy: Resources for Individuals and Families Exploring Social Change Giving.* San Diego: National Network of Grantmakers, 1997.

Smith, Huston. *The Religions of Man.* New York: HarperCollins, 1987.

Taylor, Don, and Jeanne Smalling Archer. *Up Against the Wal-Marts: How Your Business Can Prosper in the Shadow of the Retail Giants.* New York: Amacom, 1994.

Tieger, Paul, and Barbara Barron-Tieger. *Do What You Are: Discover the Perfect Career for You through the Secrets of Personality Type.* Boston: Little, Brown, 1995.

Tobias, Andrew. *The Only Investment Guide You'll Ever Need.* San Diego: Harcourt Brace Publishing, 1996.

Train, John. *The Money Masters: Nine Great Investors: Their Winning Strategies and How You Can Apply Them.* New York: Penguin Books, 1980.

Tyson, Eric. *Personal Finance for Dummies.* San Mateo, Calif.: IDG Books Worldwide, 1994.

Waldman, Mark. *The Way of Real Wealth.* San Francisco: Hazelden/ Harper, 1993.

Warner, Ralph. *Get a Life: You Don't Need a Million to Retire Well.* Berkeley, Calif.: Nolo Press, 1997.

Weatherford, Jack. *The History of Money.* New York: Crown Publishers, 1997.

Weil, Andrew. *Natural Health, Natural Medicine.* Boston: Houghton Mifflin, 1990.

———. *Spontaneous Healing.* New York: Knopf, 1995.

Wilber, Ken. *A Brief History of Everything.* Boston: Shambhala Publications, 1996.

———. *Up from Eden.* Boston: Shambhala Publications, 1986.

Wilson, Alex, and John Morrill. *Consumer Guide to Home Energy Savings.* Washington, D.C.: American Council for an Energy-Efficient Economy, 1993.

Woodrow, Peter. *Clearness: Processes for Supporting Individuals and Groups in Decision Making.* Philadelphia: New Society Publishers, 1984.

ACKNOWLEDGMENTS

Anyone who writes for a public audience knows how invaluable it is to have a sharp reader review your initial drafts. These editing angels point out incoherent sentences, inconsistent sentiments, and mistimed jokes—generally helping to keep your foot out of your mouth before anyone else sees. My main helpmate is my wife, Margaret, whose gentle heart and sensitive b.s. detector helped steer me toward more lucid shores. Beth Umland, friend, sister-in-law, advanced soul, and first-rate editor, provided crucial insight, working as an ace reliever on those sections I struggled with most.

Other helpful readers include my brother, Joe Glickman, and Chris Widney.

My agent, Barbara Moulton, was the catalyst for *The Mindful Money Guide* and its faithful advocate. She was kind enough to connect me to Susan Randol at Ballantine Books. Susan has been a pleasure to work with and had crucial input in shaping this book.

The librarians at Brattleboro Memorial and the Dover Free Library deserve my gratitude for ordering books, extending due dates over the phone, filing interlibrary loan requests, and allowing me to take out practically every financial book in southern Vermont. I have yet to meet a librarian who didn't have at least a touch of the saint in him or her, but I want especially to thank Richard Shuldiner, Vicki Wood, Pat Avery, and Jeanne Walsh.

Generous and helpful experts who deserve recognition include Meir Statman, professor of finance at Santa Clara University; Jack Brill, an investment adviser in San Diego and coauthor of *Investing from the Heart*; insurance adviser Bob Dreizler of Sacramento, California; Mark Kantorwitz, who runs the college financial aid mega Web site, the Financial Aid Information Page (www.finaid.org); and especially Anne Doyle, director of planned giving at the Environmental Defense Fund. A colleague at a "rival" charity recommended Ms. Doyle as a planned-giving whiz. She proved to be just that—and munificent to boot. Ms. Doyle reviewed the will-and-trust section in *The Mindful Money Guide,* even though she knew me only as a voice on the phone.

Thanks also to Tience Shea, Dede Cummings, and Clay Turnbull, my *Green Living* coworkers who kept the journal going even when they didn't have my full attention.

Last, please note that although there are a few occasions in *The Mindful Money Guide* when I take exception to advice in Joe Dominguez and Vicki Robin's bestseller *Your Money or Your Life,* I appreciate the positive influence their book has had and have great respect for them personally. (Both have donated all their book royalties to charity.)

INDEX

ABOUT THE AUTHOR

In 1983, after graduating Phi Beta Kappa from Northwestern University, MARSHALL GLICKMAN headed to Wall Street not with a career in mind, but a plan: his goal was to save $100,000 in three years—an amount that was enough to provide financial freedom to pursue his interests even if they didn't pay well, but not so much that he'd get sidetracked from more idealistic pursuits. Three years later, having managed $17 million of client assets at Shearson Lehman Brothers, he "retired" at the age of twenty-four with a $135,000 nest egg.

Since then Marshall has traveled, done numerous meditation retreats, been an environmental activist, renovated houses, and worked as a freelance writer. His articles have appeared in many publications, including *The New York Times Magazine*, *The Washington Post*, the *Chicago Tribune*, and *Mother Earth News*. He now lives with his wife and two daughters in South Newfane, Vermont, where he is the editor and publisher of the environmental magazine *Green Living*. He is also the treasurer and financial chairperson of the Brattleboro Food Co-op, a $7 million a year natural foods cooperative.